BEST OF THE
AIR FRYER

THE AUSTRALIAN
Women's Weekly

BEST OF THE
AIR FRYER

THE AUSTRALIAN WOMEN'S WEEKLY TEST KITCHEN
TEST KITCHEN TESTED

CONTENTS

SUPER EASY GUIDE TO AIR FRYERS

HOW THEY WORK

The air fryer is renowned for replicating the crisp texture of deep-fried foods using a fraction of the oil. This amped-up benchtop convection oven works by pushing hot air around food; the rapid circulation of air in the confined space helps to make food crisp, just like deep-frying but with much less oil. For example, air-fried hot chips contain just 4–6g fat versus 17g for the deep-fried equivalent.

BASKET AIR FRYERS These compact versions range in capacity from 3–4 litres to 6–7 litres and typically retail for under $150. With this style, the base of the handled basket is perforated and slightly elevated from the base of the pan, which collects oil drippings and cooking juices. While they are nifty they do not allow for large volumes of food, and you will not be able to cook an entire family meal in them.

OVEN AIR FRYERS These larger versions of air fryers (11 litres) open like an oven with a door. They offer the convenience of a compact oven with the benefits of an air fryer, and for a single person or couple could even suffice as their only cooking medium. These appliances come equipped with two or three wire racks for shelves, which allow for a variety of foods to be cooked at the same time. They also include additional functions, such as a low-temperature mode for dehydrating and a defrost mode for thawing food. As well, they come with pre-set functions for cooking foods like chips, chops, prawns, drumsticks and steaks. The clear oven door allows you to see how the cooking is progressing without the need to open it, keeping the temperature stable inside. Naturally, with these additional benefits, the price tag for these larger appliances is higher, ranging from the low hundreds to several hundred dollars. For this book we've used popular well-priced and mid-sized 5.3-litre and 7-litre models. We have also used the dehydrator function of a larger 11-litre 3-in-1 air fryer. If you have a larger appliance you will be able to cook larger amounts of food, while for a smaller one you will need to decrease quantities accordingly to fit in your appliance.

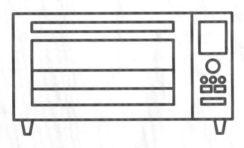

THE DIFFERENT TYPES OF AIR FRYERS

There are many different sizes and shapes of air fryers available, from compact spaceship-looking styles, which sit upright and have a deep pull-out drawer, to air fryers that look like mini ovens. These are also designed to sit on a benchtop, but they are less compact and more comparable in size to a microwave oven.

SAFETY

Before using your air fryer, read the manufacturer's instructions for your appliance.

Air fryers can get hot, so allow sufficient space on the benchtop around it. The vent at the back extracts steam, and with it grease, so you will find that you will need to wipe down the surface behind your air fryer.

Once the basket is pulled out of the appliance, treat it like it has come out of the oven – it will be hot! Take care when adding and removing items from the air fryer basket.

It is also important to clean your appliance after every use, both the inner basket and the outer pan, to remove grease, as otherwise the appliance will smoke and any small trapped pieces of food will burn.

FRYING

Air fryers excel at crisping dry ingredients, but where they don't work well is for foods with wet batters – the batter will simply stick rather than get crispy. It is also not just a case of popping food into the air fryer instead of into hot oil in a pan. The cooking method needs to be adapted to create a comparable result.

THE OTHER STUFF

The air fryer is far more than a single-use appliance for making crunchy, crispy chips. For starters, it helps to think past the name, which is a bit of a misnomer. The appliance is not a deep fryer at all and actually offers many of the benefits an oven does.

Its major limitation is the interior capacity; be sure that the dish or dishes you plan to use in your air fryer are heatproof and will fit in the appliance with room for air to circulate. Avoid any that are too tall and will come in contact with the top element of the appliance, otherwise they will burn.

If you are using the appliance to bake, avoid very light-textured or liquidy batters, as the vortex created by the appliance is strong enough to make the batter spit or create a volcanic-looking top on your baked item.

Keep an eye on sugary mixtures, as browning these in an air fryer will be accelerated.

ACCESSORIES

RACKS Most basket-style air fryers come equipped with at least one basic circular rack. Also useful is a toast rack to assist with bread slices sitting upright.

PANS Investing in cake pans that fit in your appliance will enable you to get the most out of it. Many small conventional pans will fit. Muffin pans for standard ovens won't fit, so buy a circular tray with muffin inserts.

UTENSILS While most everyday kitchen utensils like tongs, spatulas and lifters can be used in the air fryer, it is worth investing in ones with silicone ends, if you want to maintain the protective surface of your appliance.

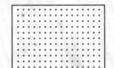

SMALL SILICONE MATS Small silicone mats are perfect for lining the base of the air fryer when cooking baked goods, as baking paper will fly up. These inexpensive mats can be bought from budget and homewares shops and can be cut to size to fit your appliance.

5 BEST FOODS TO COOK IN THE AIR FRYER

1 ROAST VEGIES

2 CRISP CHICKPEAS

3 CRUMBED FOODS

4 PIZZA & CALZONE

5 MEATBALLS & SAUSAGES

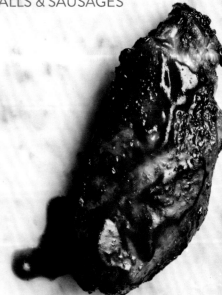

HEALTHIER SNACKS

Convenience and satisfaction are key when it comes to snacks. With the air fryer you can create healthy, tempting snacks instead of reaching for junk food filled with empty calories or laden with sugar.

CAULIFLOWER FILLO TRIANGLES

1 small onion (80g), cut into
   thin wedges
250g (8oz) cauliflower, chopped finely
2 cloves garlic, crushed
½ tsp ground turmeric
½ tsp ground ginger
¼ tsp ground cinnamon,
   plus extra to dust
extra virgin olive oil cooking spray
75g (2½oz) fetta, crumbled
2 tbsp roasted chopped almonds
2 tbsp coarsely chopped coriander
   (cilantro)
2 tbsp coarsely chopped flat-leaf parsley
12 sheets fillo pastry
to serve: lemon wedges and coriander
   (cilantro) leaves

1 Preheat a 5.3-litre air fryer to 180°C/350°F for 3 minutes.

2 Combine onion, cauliflower and garlic in a medium bowl, then sprinkle with combined spices; spray generously with oil.

3 Taking care, line the air fryer basket with baking paper. Place the cauliflower mixture in the basket; at 180°C/350°F, cook for 5 minutes until cauliflower is tender.

4 Transfer cooked cauliflower mixture to a bowl. Add fetta, almonds and herbs to the bowl; stir to combine. Cool. (Alternatively, spread mixture out on a tray and place in the freezer to chill for 5 minutes.)

5 Stack 2 sheets of pastry together, spraying between layers with oil. Cut stacked pastry lengthways into three strips. Place a heaped tablespoon of cauliflower mixture in the corner of one pastry strip, leaving a 1cm (½in) border. Fold opposite corner of pastry diagonally across filling to form a triangle; continue folding to the end of the pastry strip, retaining the triangular shape. Place, seam-side down, on a tray. Repeat with remaining pastry sheets, oil spray and cauliflower mixture to make a total of 18 fillo triangles. Spray triangles with oil; dust with extra cinnamon.

6 Place half the fillo triangles in the basket; at 180°C/350°F, cook for 10 minutes. Turn triangles over; cook for a further 10 minutes until golden. Transfer to a wire rack. Repeat cooking with remaining fillo triangles.

7 Serve fillo triangles with lemon wedges and coriander leaves.

prep + cook time 1 hour (+ cooling)
makes 18

GREEN FALAFEL & TAHINI SAUCE

2½ cups (375g) frozen edamame
(soy beans)
400g (12½oz) can chickpeas
(garbanzo beans), drained, rinsed
1 medium onion (150g), chopped
3 cloves garlic
1 cup coarsely chopped flat-leaf parsley
½ cup coarsely chopped mint
1 cup coarsely chopped coriander
(cilantro)
½ cup (750g) plain (all-purpose) flour
1 tsp fine salt
2 tsp ground cumin
1 tsp moroccan spice mix
extra virgin olive oil cooking spray
to serve: chargrilled pitta breads,
extra herbs and lemon wedges

TAHINI SAUCE
½ cup (140g) greek yoghurt
1½ tbsp tahini
1 clove garlic, crushed
2 tsp lemon juice

1 Place frozen edamame in a bowl; pour over boiling water. Stand for 1 minute; drain. Cool under cold running water. Process 2 cups edamame, the chickpeas, onion, garlic, herbs, flour, salt, cumin and spice mix until finely chopped. Shape heaped tablespoons of mixture into approximately 26 oval falafel; place on a tray lined with plastic wrap. Refrigerate for 1 hour to firm.
2 Meanwhile, to make tahini sauce, whisk ingredients in a small bowl until smooth; season to taste.
3 Preheat a 5.3-litre air fryer to 180°C/350°F for 3 minutes.

4 Spray falafel generously with oil. Taking care, place half the falafel in the air fryer basket; at 180°C/350°F, cook for 12 minutes, turning halfway through cooking time, or until golden. Transfer to a tray; cover to keep warm. Repeat cooking with the remaining falafel.
5 Fill chargrilled pitta breads with falafel, remaining edamame and extra herbs; drizzle with tahini sauce. Serve with lemon wedges.

tip Sprinkle the tahini sauce with moroccan spice mix, if you like.

prep + cook time 40 minutes
(+ refrigeration)
serves 4

SUN-DRIED TOMATO & FETTA POLENTA CHIPS

3 cups (750ml) chicken or
   vegetable stock
1 cup (170g) instant polenta
30g (1oz) butter, chopped
½ cup (40g) finely grated parmesan
90g (3oz) sun-dried tomatoes,
   no added oil, chopped finely
⅓ cup chopped basil leaves
100g (3oz) fetta, crumbled
olive oil cooking spray
to serve: sea salt flakes

SALSA VERDE
2 tbsp red wine vinegar
2 tbsp capers, chopped coarsely
1 shallot, chopped finely
½ cup basil leaves, chopped coarsely
1 cup flat-leaf parsley leaves,
   chopped coarsely
½ cup (125ml) extra virgin olive oil

1 Bring stock to the boil in a large, deep saucepan; add polenta in a thin, steady stream, whisking until the mixture comes to the boil. Reduce heat to low; cook, stirring with a long-handled wooden spoon or whisk, for 10 minutes until mixture is soft and thick. Stir in butter, parmesan, sun-dried tomato and basil.

2 Grease a deep 20cm (8in) square cake pan; line base and sides with baking paper. Spread half the polenta mixture over base of pan; scatter with half the fetta. Spread remaining polenta over fetta; scatter with remaining fetta, pressing it gently into the polenta. Cover pan. Refrigerate for 3 hours to firm.

3 Preheat a 7-litre air fryer to 200°C/400°F for 3 minutes.

4 Turn polenta out onto a board and cut into 18 chips; spray generously all over with oil.

5 Spray the air fryer basket with oil. Taking care, place polenta chips in the basket; at 200°C/400°F, cook for 15 minutes, turning halfway through cooking time, or until golden brown and crisp.

6 Meanwhile, to make salsa verde, combine ingredients in a bowl.

7 Sprinkle polenta chips with salt flakes and serve with salsa verde.

prep + cook time 50 minutes (+ refrigeration)
makes 18

TIP Smooth ricotta is available in tubs in the refrigerated section of the supermarket.

HERB-BAKED RICOTTA
WITH VEGIE DIPPERS

2 x 60g (2oz) lebanese bread rounds
20g (¾oz) butter, melted
½ tsp dried italian herb mix
500g (1lb) thick smooth ricotta
   (see tip)
1 egg, beaten lightly
⅓ cup (25g) finely grated parmesan
1 tbsp thyme leaves
¼ tsp dried chilli flakes
to serve: extra thyme leaves,
   extra virgin olive oil, baby rainbow
   carrots, baby cucumbers, radishes
   and baby gem lettuce

1 Preheat a 7-litre air fryer to 180°C/350°F for 3 minutes.

2 Brush bread rounds with butter and sprinkle with herb mix.

3 Taking care, place one of the bread rounds in the air fryer basket, then place a wire rack on top; at 180°C/350°F, cook for 3 minutes or until golden and crisp. Transfer to a plate to cool. Repeat cooking with remaining bread round. Once cooled, cut bread rounds into wedges.

4 Meanwhile, place ricotta, egg, parmesan, thyme and chilli in a medium bowl, then season; stir to combine. Divide mixture between two 300ml ovenproof baking dishes.

5 Place dishes in the air fryer basket; at 180°C/350°F, cook for 20 minutes until ricotta is golden and set. Remove dishes from the air fryer.

6 Sprinkle baked ricottas with extra thyme leaves and drizzle with olive oil. Serve warm with bread wedges, baby carrots, baby cucumbers, radishes, and lettuce.

prep + cook time 40 minutes
serves 6

HEALTHY TORTILLA CHIPS & SPECIAL GUACAMOLE

312g (10oz) packet white corn tortillas
1 tsp ground cumin
1 tsp smoked paprika
1 tsp salt flakes
extra virgin olive oil cooking spray
to serve: Tabasco chipotle sauce,
    coriander (cilantro) sprigs and
    lime wedges

SPECIAL GUACAMOLE

2 medium avocados (500g)
1 small red chilli, chopped finely
¼ tsp ground cumin
1 small clove garlic, crushed
2 tbsp lime juice
½ cup finely chopped coriander
    (cilantro)

1 Preheat a 5.3-litre air fryer to 200°C/400°F for 3 minutes.

2 Stack three tortillas on top of each other, then cut the stack into six wedges. Repeat with remaining tortillas.

3 Combine cumin, paprika and salt flakes in a small bowl.

4 Taking care, place a third of the tortilla wedges in the air fryer basket; at 200°C/400°F, cook for 7 minutes, turning halfway through cooking time, until crisp. Transfer to a platter; spray with oil and sprinkle with a third of the spice mix. Repeat with remaining tortilla wedges, oil spray and spice mix.

5 Meanwhile, to make special guacamole, using a spoon, scoop the flesh from avocados into a bowl. Add half the chilli and remaining ingredients; mash together using a potato masher or fork to form a chunky texture. Season to taste.

6 Top special guacamole with remaining chilli, chipotle sauce and coriander sprigs. Serve with tortilla chips and lime wedges.

prep it Guacamole can be made a day ahead; cover directly with plastic wrap to prevent browning and refrigerate.

keep it Tortilla chips will keep in an airtight container for up to 1 week.

prep + cook time 30 minutes
serves 4

TIP You can find spring roll wrappers in the freezer section of the supermarket. Thaw before using.

VEGETABLE SPRING ROLLS

50g (1½oz) dried rice vermicelli noodles
1 clove garlic, crushed
2 tbsp finely chopped ginger
1 shallot, sliced thinly
1 large carrot (180g), cut into
    matchsticks
2 cups (160g) shredded wombok
    (napa cabbage)
½ tsp chinese five spice powder
1 tsp sesame oil
2 tsp peanut oil
2 tbsp tamari
1 tsp cornflour (cornstarch)
10 x 21.5cm (8¾in) frozen spring roll
    wrappers, thawed (see tip)
cooking oil spray
to serve: coriander (cilantro)
    and lime wedges

1 Place vermicelli in a medium bowl of boiling water for 2 minutes until soft; drain well. Using scissors, snip noodles into shorter lengths.
2 Line the basket of a 5.3-litre air fryer with baking paper, then place garlic, ginger, shallot, carrot, wombok, five spice and oils in the basket; toss to combine. Set temperature to 180°C/350°F; cook for 5 minutes until vegetables are soft.
3 Taking care, transfer the vegetable mixture to a bowl. Combine tamari and cornflour in a small bowl. Add cornflour mixture to vegetable mixture with vermicelli; toss to combine. Cool to room temperature.

4 Place a spring roll wrapper on a flat surface. Place ¼ cup of filling in a line a third up from the bottom edge, leaving a 1.5cm (¾in) border on each side. Fold over once, then fold in the sides and roll up to enclose filling; brush the join with a little water to seal. Repeat with remaining spring roll wrappers and filling.
5 Preheat the air fryer to 180°C/350°F for 3 minutes.
6 Spray spring rolls generously with oil. Taking care, place half the rolls in the air fryer basket; at 180°C/350°F, cook for 12 minutes until golden brown. Transfer to a wire rack. Repeat cooking with remaining spring rolls.
7 Serve spring rolls with coriander and lime wedges.

serve it Try the spring rolls with the Chilli Peanut Dressing on page 101.

prep + cook time 45 minutes
makes 10

PICKLE CHIPS
WITH RANCH DIPPING SAUCE

⅓ cup (75g) plain (all-purpose) flour
⅔ cup (160ml) buttermilk
1 tbsp hot chilli sauce
2¼ cups (170g) panko (japanese)
  breadcrumbs
700g (1½lb) jar sliced bread and butter
  pickles, drained
olive oil cooking spray
½ cup (150g) whole-egg mayonnaise
½ cup (120g) light sour cream
2 tbsp chopped dill
2 tbsp chopped chives
1 small clove garlic, crushed
1 tbsp lemon juice
to serve: sea salt flakes

1 Place flour in a shallow bowl. Lightly beat buttermilk and chilli sauce in a second shallow bowl and place breadcrumbs in a third shallow bowl. Dust pickles in flour, shaking off excess, dip in buttermilk mixture, then coat in breadcrumbs; spray generously all over with oil.
2 Preheat a 7-litre air fryer to 200°C/400°F for 3 minutes.
3 Taking care, place a third of the pickles in the air fryer basket in a single layer; at 200°C/400°F, cook for 6 minutes until golden. Transfer to a plate. Repeat cooking with remaining pickles.

4 Meanwhile, to make ranch dipping sauce, combine remaining ingredients in a small bowl.
5 Sprinkle pickle chips with salt flakes and serve with ranch dipping sauce.

prep + cook time 40 minutes
serves 6

VEGETABLE
MEATZZA

500g (1lb) ground (minced) beef
½ cup (40g) grated parmesan
½ cup (35g) panko (japanese)
    breadcrumbs
½ tsp fennel seeds, crushed
¼ tsp dried thyme
1 egg, beaten lightly
1 clove garlic, crushed
⅓ cup (130g) arrabbiata pasta sauce
75g (2½oz) mozzarella, sliced thinly
½ medium zucchini (60g), sliced
½ bunch asparagus (90g), halved
    lengthways then crossways
100g (3oz) swiss brown mushrooms,
    sliced thinly
75g (2½oz) cured chorizo, sliced thinly
¼ cup basil leaves

1 Preheat a 5.3-litre air fryer to 200°C/400°F for 3 minutes.

2 Combine beef, parmesan, breadcrumbs, fennel, thyme, egg and garlic in a bowl; season.

3 Cut out a 22cm (9in) round from a piece of baking paper. Press mince mixture over baking paper round to form an 18cm (7¼in) round.

4 Taking care, lower the meatzza base, on the paper, into the air fryer basket; at 200°C/400°F, cook for 8 minutes until cooked through.

5 Carefully lift meatzza base, on the paper, from the basket; drain off liquid.

6 Spread meatzza base with pasta sauce; top with mozzarella, zucchini, asparagus, mushroom and chorizo. Lower meatzza, on the paper, back into the air fryer basket; at 200°C/400°F, cook for 10 minutes until vegetables and chorizo are cooked through.

7 Serve meatzza immediately, topped with basil.

prep + cook time 30 minutes
serves 2

GREEK FETTA & OREGANO FRIES

prep + cook time 15 minutes **serves** 4

Preheat a 5.3-litre air fryer to 200°C/400°F for 3 minutes. Place 700g (1½lb) frozen fries in the air fryer basket with 8 unpeeled cloves garlic, then spray with cooking oil; at 200°C/400°F, cook for 10 minutes, turning halfway through cooking time, or until fries are golden. Tip fries into a large bowl. Crumble over 100g (3oz) greek fetta and sprinkle with 1 tsp salt flakes and 1 tsp dried oregano; toss to combine.

HALOUMI FRIES

prep + cook time 15 minutes **serves** 4

Cut 2 x 225g (7oz) blocks of haloumi horizontally into three slices each. Cut each slice into three 'fries'; you will have 18 in total. Combine ½ cup plain (all-purpose) flour, 1 tsp each ground cumin and ground coriander, and ½ tsp smoked paprika in a bowl. Preheat a 5.3-litre air fryer to 200°C/400°F for 3 minutes. Spray the air fryer basket with cooking oil. Spray haloumi fries with cooking oil, then coat in flour mixture. Place haloumi fries in the basket in a single layer; at 200°C/400°F, cook for 5 minutes until fries are golden. Serve with greek yoghurt dipping sauce (see recipe below).

FRIES TO FIGHT FOR

ZUCCHINI FRIES

prep + cook time 30 minutes **serves** 4

Cut 3 large zucchini (450g) in half crossways. Cut zucchini halves into 1cm (½in) thick 'fries'. Combine ⅔ cup ground almonds (or panko breadcrumbs), ½ cup finely grated parmesan, 1 tsp each smoked paprika and finely chopped rosemary or oregano, and a pinch of ground chilli in a bowl. Preheat a 5.3 litre air fryer to 200°C/400°F for 3 minutes. Toss zucchini fries with 2 tbsp extra virgin olive oil, then coat in almond mixture. Place half the zucchini fries in the air fryer basket in a single layer; at 200°C/400°F, cook for 10 minutes, turning halfway through cooking time, until fries are golden. Transfer to a plate; cover to keep warm. Repeat with remaining zucchini fries. Season to taste. Serve with greek yoghurt dipping sauce (see recipe right).

GREEK YOGHURT DIPPING SAUCE

prep time 5 minutes **makes** 1¼ cups

Combine 1¼ cups (350g) greek yoghurt, 1 tsp finely grated lemon rind, 1 smashed clove garlic, 2 tbsp finely chopped dill and 2 tbsp finely chopped mint; season taste. Remove the garlic clove when ready to serve.

tip Use just one herb in the recipe, if preferred.

greek fetta & oregano fries

haloumi fries

zucchini fries

greek yoghurt dipping sauce

ZUCCHINI BALLS WITH LEMON YOGHURT

700g (1½lb) zucchini, grated coarsely
2 tsp coarse cooking salt
1 egg, beaten lightly
½ cup (120g) fresh firm ricotta,
  crumbled
⅓ cup (25g) finely grated parmesan
1 cup (100g) packaged breadcrumbs
½ cup finely chopped flat-leaf parsley
3 green onions (scallions), sliced thinly
olive oil cooking spray
¾ cup (200g) greek yoghurt
1 small clove garlic, crushed
2 tsp finely grated lemon rind
1 tbsp lemon juice
to serve: sea salt flakes

1 Place zucchini in a colander and sprinkle with salt; stand for 20 minutes. Using your hands, squeeze zucchini very firmly to remove excess liquid; transfer to a large bowl.
2 Add egg, ricotta, parmesan, breadcrumbs, parsley and green onion to bowl, then season; stir until well combined. With damp hands, shape heaped tablespoons of zucchini mixture into balls; place on a tray lined with baking paper. Spray all over with oil.
3 Preheat a 7-litre air fryer to 180°C/350°F for 3 minutes. Cut out a 22cm (9in) round from a piece of baking paper.

4 Taking care, line the air fryer basket with the baking paper round. Place zucchini balls in the basket; at 180°C/350°F, cook for 25 minutes, turning after 15 minutes of cooking time, until golden and cooked through.
5 Meanwhile, to make lemon yoghurt, combine remaining ingredients in a small bowl.
6 Sprinkle zucchini balls with salt flakes and serve with lemon yoghurt.

prep + cook time 45 minutes (+ standing)
makes 24

WONTON
CRISPS WITH
PINEAPPLE
& PEANUT SALAD

270g (8½oz) packet wonton skins
olive oil cooking spray
1 small red onion (100g)
¼ cup (60ml) lime juice
900g (1¾lb) pineapple
4 baby cucumbers
1 long red chilli
2 tbsp brown sugar
1 tbsp soy sauce
2 tbsp mint leaves
2 tbsp coriander (cilantro) leaves
2 tbsp asian fried shallots
¼ cup (35g) roasted peanuts
to serve: lime wedges

1 Preheat a 5.3-litre air fryer to 180°C/350°F for 3 minutes.

2 Working with 10 wonton skins at a time, spray both sides with oil. Taking care, remove the air fryer basket from the air fryer pan. Carefully place the wonton skins on the base of the pan in a single layer, then reinsert the basket back into the pan to cover the skins (doing this will prevent the wonton skins from flying around inside the appliance); at 180°C/350°F, cook for 4 minutes until golden, blistered and crisp. Repeat cooking with remaining wonton skins and oil spray.

3 Meanwhile to make salad, thinly slice onion and toss with a little salt and the lime juice in a small bowl. Peel, core and thinly slice pineapple; place in a medium bowl. Thinly slice cucumbers into rounds. Halve chilli, remove seeds and chop finely. Add cucumber and chilli to pineapple. Add pickled onion to pineapple, reserving any lime juice in the bowl. Stir sugar, soy sauce and 1 tablespoon water into reserved lime juice to make a dressing. Add dressing and herbs to the pineapple salad; toss gently to combine.

4 Top crisp wonton skins with pineapple salad, fried shallots and peanuts. Serve with lime wedges.

prep + cook time 40 minutes
serves 4

MANGO STRAWBERRY FIUIT LEATHER

2 medium mangoes (860g), chopped coarsely (see tip)
250g (8oz) fresh strawberries, halved
2 tbsp caster (superfine) sugar

1 Remove the three racks from an 11-litre air fryer and cover with baking paper.

2 Blend or process mango until smooth. Spread mango evenly over baking paper on each rack to form a thin layer.

3 Blend or process strawberries and sugar until smooth. Dollop strawberry mixture onto mango layers. Gently spread strawberry mixture over mango using the back of a spoon.

4 Place the racks back in the air fryer. Set to dehydration setting and temperature to 80°C/175°F; dehydrate for 3 hours, rotating racks every hour, or until fruit is shiny, dried but still slightly tacky to touch. Remove racks from the air fryer. Leave fruit leather on racks to cool.

5 Using kitchen scissors, cut each fruit leather sheet, still on the baking paper, into three wide strips. Keeping paper attached, roll fruit leathers up tightly and wrap in plastic wrap. Store in an airtight container in a cool, dry place.

tip You will need 500g (1lb) mango flesh. When mangoes aren't in season, you can use frozen mango instead. Drying time may vary.

prep + cook time 3 hours 20 minutes (+ cooling)
makes 9 strips

37

CRISPY
PEPPERONI
FLAVOURED
PEAS & BEANS

---

2 x 400g (12½oz) cans chickpeas
(garbanzo beans), drained, rinsed
200g (6½oz) frozen edamame
(soy beans), thawed
⅓ cup (80ml) extra virgin olive oil
2 tsp garlic granules (see tip)
2 tsp fennel seeds
2 tsp dried chilli flakes
2 tsp onion powder
2 tsp smoked paprika
1 tsp salt flakes
¼ cup (50g) pepitas (pumpkin seed
kernels) (optional)

1 Preheat a 5.3-litre air fryer to 180°C/350°F for 3 minutes.

2 Place chickpeas on a tray lined with paper towel; pat with more paper towel until well dried. Repeat with edamame on fresh paper towel.

3 Toss chickpeas with 2 tablespoons of the oil in a large bowl. Combine garlic granules, fennel seeds, chilli flakes, onion powder, paprika and salt flakes in a small bowl. Sprinkle half the spice mix over chickpeas.

4 Taking care, place the chickpeas in the air fryer basket; at 180°C/350°F, cook for 15 minutes, turning twice during cooking time, or until crisp and golden. Add the pepitas, if using, 2 minutes before the end of cooking time. Transfer to a clean bowl to cool.

5 Combine edamame, remaining oil and remaining spice mix in a bowl. Place edamame in the air fryer basket; at 180°C/350°F, cook for 12 minutes, turning twice during cooking time, or until crisp and darkened. Transfer edamame to bowl with chickpeas to cool.

keep it Crisp peas and beans mixture will keep in an airtight container for up to 1 week.

prep + cook time 40 minutes
makes 3 cups

TIP Garlic granules, sometimes sold as granulated garlic, are sold in small packets or jars alongside other spices in the supermarket.

TIP Lightly crush All-Bran and cornflakes using your hands.

CRANBERRY ALMOND GO BARS

2 tbsp LSA mix
1½ tbsp cornflour (cornstarch)
1 cup (90g) rolled oats
½ cup (35g) All-Bran, crushed lightly
   (see tip)
1 cup (40g) cornflakes, crushed lightly
   (see tip)
½ cup (40g) desiccated coconut
½ cup (80g) sultanas
⅓ cup (45g) dried sweetened
   cranberries
⅓ cup (45g) slivered almonds
¼ cup (40g) pepita and
   sunflower seed mix
2 tbsp black chia seeds
1 tsp ground cinnamon
125g (4oz) virgin coconut oil
¼ cup (90g) honey
¼ cup (60ml) maple syrup
100g (3oz) dark (semi-sweet)
   chocolate, melted

1 Grease a 20cm (8in) square cake pan; line base and sides with baking paper.
2 Process LSA mix, cornflour and ¾ cup oats in a food processor until fine. Combine oat mixture, remaining oats, the All-Bran, cornflakes, coconut, sultanas, cranberries, almonds, seed mix, chia seeds and cinnamon in a large bowl; mix well.
3 Stir coconut oil, honey and maple syrup in a small saucepan over low heat until smooth; stir into oat mixture until combined. Press mixture firmly into cake pan; cover tightly with foil.
4 Preheat a 7-litre air fryer to 150°C/300°F for 3 minutes.

5 Taking care, place cake pan in the air fryer basket; at 150°C/300°F, cook for 20 minutes. Remove foil; cook for a further 15 minutes until golden. Remove cake pan from the air fryer. Cool.
6 Once cool, place cake pan in the fridge for 2 hours or until slab is firm. Remove slab from the pan and cut into 12 bars. Drizzle bars with melted chocolate. Refrigerate for a further 20 minutes or until chocolate sets.

keep it Bars will keep in an airtight container in the fridge for up to 1 week.

prep + cook time 55 minutes (+ refrigeration)
makes 12

CINNAMON TORTILLA CRISPS WITH FRUITY YOGHURT SAUCES

6 x 20cm (8in) flour tortillas
50g (1½oz) butter, melted
1 tsp ground cinnamon
2 tbsp caster (superfine) sugar
60g (2oz) raspberries
1 tbsp lemon curd
170g (5½oz) tub vanilla yoghurt
60g (2oz) blackberries
170g (5½oz) tub passionfruit yoghurt

1 Preheat a 7-litre air fryer to 180°C/350°F for 3 minutes.

2 Brush one side of each tortilla with butter. Combine cinnamon and sugar in a small bowl. Sprinkle buttered side of tortillas with the cinnamon sugar. Stack the tortillas on top of each other; cut into 12 wedges.

3 Taking care, place half the tortilla wedges in the air fryer basket in a single layer, then place a wire rack on top (this will stop the wedges from flying up); at 180°C/350°F, cook for 4 minutes, turning halfway through cooking time, until golden and crisp. Transfer to a tray to cool. Repeat cooking with remaining tortilla wedges.

4 Meanwhile, to make fruity yoghurt sauces, crush raspberries using the back of a fork, then stir in lemon curd and vanilla yoghurt until combined; transfer to a bowl. Crush blackberries using the back of a fork, then stir into passionfruit yoghurt until combined; transfer to a bowl.

5 Serve tortilla crisps with yoghurt sauces.

prep + cook time 15 minutes
serves 4

BACON & LEEK FRITTATAS

1 tbsp extra virgin olive oil
3 centre-cut bacon rashers (105g), chopped finely
½ small leek (100g), sliced thinly
2 eggs
⅓ cup (80ml) pouring cream
½ cup (60g) grated pizza cheese
to serve: sea salt flakes (optional)

1 Grease a 12-hole mini (1 tablespoon/20ml) muffin pan.

2 Heat oil in a medium frying pan; cook bacon, stirring, for 3 minutes or until browned lightly. Add leek; cook, stirring, for 5 minutes or until leek softens and bacon is crisp. Cool for 2 minutes.

3 Preheat a 7-litre air fryer to 180°C/350°F for 3 minutes.

4 Spoon bacon mixture into pan holes. Lightly whisk eggs and cream in a jug, then season; stir in 2 tablespoons of the cheese. Pour mixture into pan holes; sprinkle with remaining cheese.

5 Taking care, gently lower muffin pan into the air fryer basket; at 180°C/350°F, cook for 5 minutes. Cover muffin pan with greased foil; cook for a further 5 minutes until frittatas are golden and cooked through. Remove muffin pan from the air fryer. Leave frittatas in pan for 5 minutes before turning, top-side up, onto a wire rack to cool.

6 Sprinkle frittatas with salt flakes to serve, if you like.

prep + cook time 30 minutes
makes 12

SRIRACHA VEGETABLE TEMPURA

1 bunch asparagus (175g)
1 head broccoli (400g)
1 medium carrot (120g)
150g (4½oz) oyster mushrooms
⅔ cup (100g) self-raising flour
½ tsp fine salt
1 egg
1 tbsp sriracha chilli sauce
¾ cup (180ml) chilled sparkling water
2¼ cups (185g) panko (japanese) breadcrumbs
100ml extra virgin olive oil
to serve: tamari or ponzu sauce, finely chopped red chilli and toasted sesame seeds

1 Trim asparagus. Cut broccoli into florets. Cut carrot into 5mm (¼in) slices on a diagonal. Separate mushrooms, if necessary.

2 Combine flour and salt in a large bowl. Place egg, sriracha and sparkling water in a jug; whisk to combine. Add egg mixture to flour mixture; whisk until just combined.

3 Preheat a 5.3-litre air fryer to 180°C/350°F for 3 minutes. Line a tray with baking paper and top a second tray with a wire rack.

4 Place breadcrumbs in a bowl; drizzle over oil. Using your fingertips, rub the oil into the crumbs until well combined. Working with one vegetable piece at a time, dip in batter, allowing excess to drip off, then coat in breadcrumb mixture; place on lined tray. Continue coating until you have 6–8 vegetable pieces ready to cook.

5 Taking care, place the vegetables in the air fryer basket in a single layer; at 180°C/350°F, cook for 5 minutes, turning halfway through cooking time, or until golden brown. Transfer to the wire rack over tray.

6 Repeat coating and cooking remaining vegetable pieces in four more batches.

7 Serve vegetable tempura with tamari sprinkled with finely chopped red chilli and toasted sesame seeds.

prep + cook time 40 minutes
serves 4

dried watermelon

dried pineapple

dried apple

dried kiwifruit

DRIED PINEAPPLE

Lightly spray two of the included racks of an 11-litre air fryer with olive oil cooking spray. Cut a pineapple in half crossways through the middle (reserve the other half for another use). Peel then remove the core with an apple corer. Thinly slice pineapple into 2mm-thick rings. Arrange rings over racks in a single layer. Taking care, place racks in the air fryer. Set air fryer to dehydration setting and set temperature to 70°C/160°F; cook for 4 hours, rotating racks halfway through cooking time, or until pineapple is dried. Remove racks from the air fryer. Leave pineapple on racks to cool. Store in an airtight container in a cool, dry place for up to 2 weeks.

DRIED APPLE

Lightly spray two of the included racks of an 11-litre air fryer with olive oil cooking spray. Using a mandoline or V-slicer, thinly slice 2 red apples into 1–2mm-thick slices. Arrange apple slices over racks in a single layer. Taking care, place racks in the air fryer. Set air fryer to dehydration setting and set temperature to 70°C/160°F; cook for 4 hours, rotating racks halfway through cooking time, or until apple is dried and crisp. Remove racks from the air fryer. Leave apple on racks to cool. Store in an airtight container in a cool, dry place for up to 2 weeks.

prep + cook time
4 hours 15 minutes (+ cooling)

DEHYDRATED SNACKS

DRIED WATERMELON

Lightly spray two of the included racks of an 11-litre air fryer with olive oil cooking spray. Using a sharp knife, cut an 800g (1½lb) wedge of watermelon into 2–3mm-thick slices. Arrange watermelon slices over racks in a single layer. Taking care, place racks in the air fryer. Set air fryer to dehydration setting and set temperature to 70°C/160°F; cook for 4 hours, rotating racks halfway through cooking time, or until watermelon is dried. Remove racks from the air fryer. Leave watermelon on racks to cool. Store in an airtight container in a cool, dry place for up to 2 weeks.

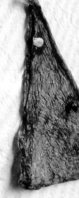

DRIED KIWIFRUIT

Lightly spray two of the included racks of an 11-litre air fryer with olive oil cooking spray. Peel 4 kiwifruit, then thinly slice into 2mm-thick slices. Arrange kiwifruit slices over racks in a single layer. Taking care, place racks in the air fryer. Set air fryer to dehydration setting and set temperature to 70°C/160°F; cook for 4 hours, rotating racks halfway through cooking time, or until kiwifruit is dried. Remove racks from the air fryer. Leave kiwifruit on racks to cool. Store in an airtight container in a cool, dry place for up to 2 weeks.

4
WAYS

SPINACH & FETTA TWISTS

250g (8oz) frozen spinach, thawed
2 sheets frozen puff pastry, just thawed
100g (3oz) fetta, crumbled
½ cup (40g) finely grated parmesan
cooking oil spray

1 Place spinach in a fine sieve; squeeze out excess liquid. Coarsely chop spinach, then pat dry between sheets of paper towel.

2 Place a pastry sheet on a tray lined with baking paper. Top with half the spinach, half the combined cheeses, then the remaining sheet of pastry; scatter over remaining spinach and cheeses. Cut pastry stack in half; place one half on top of the other half and press down firmly. Place pastry stack in the freezer for 5 minutes to firm, then cut crossways into 24 strips. Pinch one end of a strip, then twist from that end to the other end until 20cm (8in) long, pinch other end to seal. Repeat twisting with remaining strips.

3 Preheat a 5.3-litre air fryer to 200°C/400°F for 3 minutes.

4 Spray the air fryer basket with oil. Taking care, place half the twists in the basket; at 200°C/400°F, cook for 5 minutes until golden brown and cooked through. Transfer to a wire rack to cool. Repeat cooking with remaining twists.

keep it Twists will keep in an airtight container for up to 3 days.

prep + cook time 30 minutes
makes 24

SWAP IT Get crisping with other vegies: try sweet potato and jerusalem artichokes. Jerusalem artichokes pop up around winter and look rather unimpressive, but don't let that put you off as they taste amazing.

VEGIE CHIPS

3 large orange carrots (540g)
3 medium purple carrots (360g)
3 medium parsnips (750g)
1 medium beetroot (175g)
extra virgin olive oil cooking spray
to serve: salt flakes

1 Preheat a 5.3-litre air fryer to 120°C/250°F for 3 minutes.

2 Cut carrots, parsnips and beetroot in half lengthways. Using a mandoline or V-slicer, slice, cut-side down, into 2mm-thick slices.

3 Taking care, place purple carrot and beetroot slices in the air fryer basket; at 120°C/250°F, cook for 30 minutes, stirring halfway through cooking time and separating the slices, or until crisp. Transfer purple carrot chips to a tray; cover to keep warm. Cook beetroot chips for a further 5 minutes; transfer to tray with purple carrot chips. Spray chips with oil and sprinkle with salt flakes. Cool.

4 Repeat cooking with parsnip slices, then orange carrot slices, cooking at 120°C/250°F for 25 minutes each. Add to tray with purple carrot and beetroot chips; spray with oil and sprinkle with more salt flakes or one of the seasoning variations.

seasoning variations
fennel & chilli Crush 2 teaspoons fennel seeds in a mortar and pestle until coarsely ground; stir in 1 teaspoon dried chilli flakes.
sumac & thyme Combine 1 teaspoon sumac and 2 teaspoons chopped thyme.
smoked paprika Combine 1 teaspoon smoked paprika and 1 teaspoon onion powder.

keep it Vegie chips will keep in an airtight container for up to 4 days.

prep + cook time 1¾ hours
serves 6

PEAR & RICOTTA FRITTERS

¼ cup (60ml) buttermilk
1 egg
125g (4oz) smooth ricotta
2 tbsp caster (superfine) sugar
½ tsp ground cinnamon
¾ cup (105g) self-raising flour
1 large corella pear (200g),
    peeled, grated
olive oil cooking spray
1 cup (280g) vanilla yoghurt
2 tbsp honey

1 Preheat a 7-litre air fryer to 200°C/400°F for 3 minutes.

2 Whisk the buttermilk, egg, ricotta, sugar and cinnamon in a medium bowl until well combined. Sift flour over ricotta mixture; mix to combine. Fold in pear.

3 Taking care, line the air fryer basket with baking paper. Drop six heaped tablespoons of fritter mixture onto the paper 2cm (¾in) apart. Using the back of a spoon, smooth the surface of the fritters to flatten slightly, then spray with oil; at 200°C/400°F, cook for 8 minutes, turning halfway through cooking time, until golden and cooked through. Transfer to a plate; cover loosely with foil to keep warm. Repeat cooking with remaining fritter mixture and oil spray to make 12 fritters in total.

4 Serve fritters warm, dolloped with yoghurt and drizzled with honey.

prep + cook time 30 minutes
makes 12

BBQ SPICED ALMONDS

1 egg white
2 tsp smoked paprika
1 tsp mexican chilli powder
2 tsp sea salt flakes
1 tsp ground cumin
1 tsp garlic powder
2 tbsp caster (superfine) sugar
3 cups (480g) almond kernels

1 Preheat a 7-litre air fryer to 180°C/350°F for 3 minutes.

2 Whisk egg white in a large bowl until frothy; stir in paprika, chilli powder, salt, cumin, garlic powder and sugar until combined. Add almonds; stir to coat.

3 Taking care, place almonds in the air fryer basket; at 160°C/325°F, cook for 6–8 minutes, stirring halfway through cooking time, or until golden and toasted. Transfer to a plate to cool.

4 Once cooled, store almonds in an airtight container for up to 2 weeks.

prep + cook time 15 minutes
makes 3 cups

FAVOURITE DINNERS

When you have a family to feed or are ravenous after arriving home from work, getting dinner on the table fast is the priority. The air fryer, with its fast heating and rapid air circulation, makes this possible.

CHEESE BURGERS

500g (1lb) minced (ground) beef
1 egg
¾ cup (75g) panko (japanese)
   breadcrumbs
2 tbsp barbecue sauce
1 tsp smoked paprika
1 clove garlic, crushed
¼ cup (70g) low-sugar tomato sauce
   (ketchup)
olive oil cooking spray
4 slices cheddar
4 centre-cut bacon rashers (140g)
4 large brioche buns (400g)
2 tbsp whole-egg mayonnaise
4 baby cos (romaine) lettuce leaves
⅓ cup (40g) burger pickles
to serve: sweet potato chips

1 Using your hands, combine beef, egg, breadcrumbs, barbecue sauce, paprika, garlic and 1 tablespoon of the tomato sauce in a large bowl, then season; mix well. Shape mixture into four patties the same size as the brioche buns; ensure they will all fit in the air fryer basket. Spray all over with oil.
2 Preheat a 7-litre air fryer to 180°C/350°F for 3 minutes.
3 Spray the air fryer basket with oil. Taking care, place patties in the basket; at 180°C/350°F, cook for 10 minutes, turning halfway through cooking time, or until browned and cooked through. Transfer to a plate and top each with a slice of cheddar; cover loosely with foil to keep warm.

4 Taking care, arrange bacon in the air fryer basket. Reset the temperature to 200°C/400°F; cook for 5 minutes until crisp.
5 Split and toast brioche buns. Spread bun bases with mayonnaise, then top with lettuce, patties, bacon, pickles and remaining tomato sauce; sandwich together with bun tops.
6 Serve cheeseburgers with sweet potato chips.

prep + cook time 30 minutes
serves 4

MATCH IT Italian-style Rice Salad, page 132.

SWEET POTATO
PARMIS

4 small orange sweet potatoes (1kg),
　scrubbed
2 tbsp extra virgin olive oil
⅓ cup (85g) tomato pasta sauce
125g (4oz) shaved leg ham
⅔ cup (70g) coarsely grated mozzarella
2 tbsp finely grated parmesan
to serve: extra finely grated parmesan
　and basil leaves

1 Pierce sweet potatoes all over with a small, sharp knife or fork; rub with oil and season. Wrap each sweet potato individually in foil.
2 Preheat a 7-litre air fryer to 200°C/400°F for 3 minutes.
3 Taking care, place sweet potatoes in the air fryer basket in a single layer; at 200°C/400°F, cook for 50 minutes, turning halfway through cooking time, or until tender. Transfer to a plate; remove and discard foil.
4 Cut sweet potatoes in half lengthways, being careful not to cut all the way through; open out so flesh side is facing up. Spoon over pasta sauce, then top with ham and cheeses.

5 Taking care, place sweet potato parmis in the air fryer basket in a single layer; at 200°C/400°F, cook for 5 minutes or until cheese topping is golden and melted.
6 Serve sweet potato parmis topped with extra finely grated parmesan and basil leaves.

prep + cook time 1 hour 10 minutes
serves 4

SAUSAGE & VEGIE TRAY BAKE

1 red onion, cut into wedges
1 medium red capsicum (bell pepper)
   (200g), cut into thick strips
1 medium yellow capsicum (bell pepper)
   (200g), cut into thick strips
400g (12½oz) kent pumpkin, skin on,
   cut into 1cm (½in) wedges
olive oil cooking spray
8 thick pork and fennel sausages
1 cup (260g) basil pesto
1 tbsp extra virgin olive oil

1 Preheat an 11-litre air fryer to 200°C/400°F for 3 minutes.

2 Place vegetables on two of the three air fryer racks; spray with oil. Slide racks into the top two shelves of the air fryer; at 200°C/400°F, cook for 15 minutes, turning vegetables and swapping racks halfway through cooking time. Transfer racks to the bottom two shelves of the air fryer.

3 Place sausages on the remaining rack; spray with oil. Slide the rack into the top shelf of the air fryer; at 200°C/400°F, cook for 15 minutes, turning halfway through cooking time, until sausages are cooked through and vegetables are tender.

4 Meanwhile, combine pesto and oil in a small bowl.

5 Transfer vegetables and sausages to a platter. Serve drizzled with pesto dressing.

tip For smaller air fryers, you will need to cook the vegetables in batches.

prep + cook time 45 minutes
serves 4

FISH & CHIPS

1kg (2lb) small sweet potatoes
1 tbsp extra virgin olive oil
¼ cup (35g) plain (all-purpose) flour
1 egg
1 tbsp ground cumin
1 tbsp ground coriander
1 tsp ground turmeric
2 tsp coarse cooking salt
¼ cup (40g) sesame seeds
⅔ cup (50g) panko (japanese)
  breadcrumbs
800g (1½lb) skinless flathead fillets
cooking oil spray
to serve: lime wedges

YOGHURT TARTARE
½ cup (140g) greek yoghurt
2 tsp lime juice
2 baby gherkins (30g), chopped finely
2 green onions (scallions),
  chopped finely
1 tbsp finely chopped dill

1 Preheat a 5.3-litre
air fryer to 180°C/350°F
for 3 minutes.
2 Scrub sweet potatoes,
pat dry, then cut into chips.
Place chips in a large bowl
with oil and season; mix well
to coat.
3 Taking care, place chips
in the air fryer basket;
at 180°C/350°F, cook for
15 minutes, turning halfway
through cooking time, until
golden. Transfer to a plate;
cover to keep warm.
4 Meanwhile, place flour in
a shallow bowl. Lightly beat
egg in a second shallow bowl.
Combine spices, salt, sesame
seeds and breadcrumbs in a
third shallow bowl. Dust fish
in flour, shaking off excess,
dip in egg, then coat in
breadcrumb mixture;
spray generously on both
sides with oil.

5 Taking care, place fish
in the air fryer basket;
at 180°C/350°F, cook
for 13 minutes until golden
and cooked through.
6 Meanwhile, to make
yoghurt tartare, combine
ingredients in a small bowl;
season to taste.
7 Serve fish and chips
with yoghurt tartare and
lime wedges.

swap it We used orange
sweet potatoes, but you
could use white or purple
sweet potatoes, or even
a combination of colours,
if you prefer.

prep + cook time 40 minutes
serves 4

BEEF SKEWERS WITH GARLIC TZATZIKI

You will need 8 x 22cm (8¾in) metal skewers for this recipe.

1 tbsp finely grated lemon rind
2 tbsp lemon juice
1 tsp dried oregano
1 tbsp extra virgin olive oil
3 cloves garlic, crushed
500g (1lb) beef scotch fillet,
    cut into 2.5cm (1in) pieces
1 medium red capsicum (bell pepper)
    (200g), cut into 3cm (1¼in) pieces
1 medium yellow capsicum (bell pepper)
    (200g), cut into 3cm (1¼in) pieces
220g (7oz) tub tzatziki (see tips)
to serve: salad leaves and lemon cheeks

1 Combine lemon rind and juice, oregano, oil and two-thirds of the garlic in a shallow dish; add beef and toss to coat. Thread beef and both capsicums, alternately, onto skewers.

2 Preheat a 7-litre air fryer to 200°C/400°F for 3 minutes.

3 Taking care, place skewers in the air fryer basket; at 200°C/400°F, cook for 8 minutes, turning halfway through cooking time, for medium or until cooked to your liking.

4 Meanwhile, stir remaining garlic into tzatziki in the tub; transfer to a serving bowl.

5 Place skewers on a platter. Serve with tzatziki, salad leaves and lemon cheeks.

tips If you are using a smaller air fryer, you will need to cook the skewers in batches. For homemade tzatziki, coarsely grate ½ small lebanese cucumber and squeeze out the excess liquid; combine in a bowl with ¾ cup (210g) greek yoghurt and ½ clove crushed garlic, then season.

prep + cook time 30 minutes
serves 4

MATCH IT Greek-style Potatoes, page 195.

SWAP IT
Replace all the
spices with a sachet
of taco seasoning.

JAMAICAN FISH TACOS

1 tsp ground allspice
½ tsp dried thyme
1½ tsp cayenne pepper
1 tsp ground cinnamon
1½ tbsp garlic powder
2 tbsp brown sugar
¼ cup (60ml) olive oil
800g (1½lb) firm white skinless fish
  fillets, cut into long pieces (see tip)
16 x 14cm (5½in) flour tortillas
cooking oil spray
to serve: lime cheeks

AVOCADO CREAM
2 medium avocados (500g)
½ cup (120g) sour cream
2 tbsp lime juice

SLAW
350g (11oz) green cabbage, shredded
2 cups coriander (cilantro) leaves
1 small red onion (100g), sliced thinly
1 long green chilli, seeded, sliced thinly

1 Combine allspice, thyme, cayenne pepper, cinnamon, garlic powder, sugar and oil in a medium bowl; add fish and toss to coat. Season with salt.

2 To make avocado cream, blend or process ingredients until smooth; season to taste.

3 Wrap tortillas in foil. Place in the basket of a 5.3-litre air fryer; at 180°C/350°F; cook for 5 minutes to preheat the air fryer and warm the tortillas.

4 Taking care, transfer tortillas to a plate; cover to keep warm. Spray fish with oil and place in the air fryer basket; at 180°C/350°F, cook for 8 minutes, turning halfway through cooking time, or until cooked through.

5 Meanwhile, to make slaw, combine ingredients in a bowl.

6 Fill warm tortillas with fish and slaw; top with avocado cream. Serve with lime cheeks.

tip Cut fish fillets lengthways on the diagonal into 1.5cm (¾in) wide, 12cm (4¾in) long strips.

prep it Fish can be prepared to the end of step 1 up to 4 hours ahead. Avocado cream and slaw can also be prepared up to 4 hours ahead. Refrigerate until required.

prep + cook time 25 minutes
serves 8

COCONUT HONEY PRAWNS

½ cup (75g) plain (all-purpose) flour
2 eggs
1½ cups (115g) shredded coconut
1 cup (75g) panko (japanese)
   breadcrumbs
600g (1¼lb) peeled uncooked prawns
   (shrimp), tails intact
olive oil cooking spray
to serve: steamed jasmine rice
   and steamed buk choy

HONEY SAUCE
⅓ cup (120g) honey
1 tbsp lemon juice
1 tbsp soy sauce
1 tsp finely grated ginger
1 clove garlic, crushed
½ tsp chinese five spice powder
2 tsp cornflour (cornstarch)

1 Place flour in a shallow bowl. Lightly whisk eggs in a second shallow bowl. Combine coconut and breadcrumbs in a third shallow bowl. Dust prawns in flour, shaking off excess, dip in egg, then coat in coconut mixture; place on a tray. Refrigerate for 30 minutes.

2 Meanwhile, to make honey sauce, combine honey, lemon juice, soy sauce, ginger, garlic and five spice in a small saucepan over medium heat; cook, stirring, for 2 minutes or until honey melts. Bring to the boil. Blend cornflour and 1 tablespoon water in a small cup. Whisk cornflour mixture into sauce; cook, stirring, for 2 minutes or until thickened slightly. Remove from heat; cover to keep warm.

3 Preheat a 7-litre air fryer to 200°C/400°F for 3 minutes.

4 Spray prawns generously all over with oil. Taking care, place half the prawns in the air fryer basket in a single layer; at 200°C/400°F, cook for 6 minutes, turning halfway through cooking time, until golden and just cooked through. Transfer to a plate; cover loosely with foil to keep warm. Repeat cooking with remaining prawns.

5 Serve prawns with steamed rice and steamed buk choy, drizzled with honey sauce.

prep + cook time 40 minutes (+ refrigeration)
serves 4

MATCH IT Lentil Tabbouleh, page 132.

HERBY LAMB KOFTAS WITH GREEN TAHINI

500g (1lb) minced (ground) lamb
2 tsp ground cumin
2 tsp ground coriander
1 tsp paprika
1 egg, beaten lightly
¼ cup (25g) packaged breadcrumbs
½ cup finely chopped mint
½ cup finely chopped flat-leaf parsley
olive oil cooking spray
½ cup (140g) greek yoghurt
2 tbsp tahini
2 tbsp lemon juice
to serve: grilled pitta bread rounds,
    cut into wedges

TOMATO SALAD

250g (8oz) mixed colour cherry
    tomatoes, halved
1 lebanese cucumber, sliced thickly
2 tbsp mint leaves
2 tbsp flat-leaf parsley leaves
extra virgin olive oil, to drizzle

1 Using your hands, combine lamb, cumin, coriander, paprika, egg, breadcrumbs and half each of the chopped mint and parsley in a bowl; mix well. With damp hands, shape level tablespoons of mince mixture into balls; place on a tray. Spray all over with oil.

2 Preheat a 7-litre air fryer to 180°C/350°F for 3 minutes.

3 Spray the air fryer basket with oil. Taking care, place koftas in the basket in a single layer; at 180°C/350°F, cook for 8 minutes, shaking the basket halfway through cooking time, until browned and cooked through.

4 Meanwhile, to make green tahini, combine yoghurt, tahini, lemon juice and remaining chopped mint and parsley in a small bowl.

5 To make tomato salad, combine tomatoes, cucumber, mint and parsley on a platter; drizzle with oil and season.

6 Add koftas and green tahini to platter. Serve with grilled pitta bread.

prep + cook time 35 minutes
serves 4

75

POPCORN-COATED CHICKEN WITH HONEY BBQ SAUCE

100g (3oz) packet popped
   butter popcorn
¼ cup (35g) plain (all-purpose) flour
1 tsp dried oregano
1 tsp sweet paprika
1 tsp sea salt flakes
½ tsp mustard powder
2 eggs
16 chicken tenderloins (1.2kg)
olive oil cooking spray
½ cup (140g) barbecue sauce
¼ cup (90g) honey
1 tsp dijon mustard

1 Process popcorn until coarsely chopped; transfer to a shallow bowl. Combine flour, oregano, paprika, salt flakes and mustard powder in a second shallow bowl. Lightly beat eggs in a third shallow bowl. Dust chicken in flour mixture, shaking off excess, dip in egg, then coat in popcorn; spray generously all over with oil.

2 Preheat a 7-litre air fryer to 180°C/350°F for 3 minutes.

3 Taking care, place chicken in the air fryer basket; at 180°C/350°F, cook for 15 minutes, turning halfway through cooking time, or until golden and cooked through.

4 Meanwhile, to make honey BBQ sauce, combine barbecue sauce, honey and mustard in a small bowl.

5 Serve popcorn-coated chicken with honey BBQ sauce.

prep + cook time 30 minutes
serves 4

SERVE IT You could also serve the chicken with mayonnaise swirled with sriracha chilli sauce, if you like.

BBQ
BOURBON
CHICKEN WINGS

½ cup (140g) barbecue sauce
¼ cup (60ml) bourbon
1 tbsp dijon mustard
1.5kg (3lb) chicken wing nibbles
to serve: extra barbecue sauce

1 Combine barbecue sauce, bourbon and mustard in a large bowl; add chicken and toss to coat.
2 Preheat a 7-litre air fryer to 180°C/350°F for 3 minutes.
3 Taking care, place chicken in the air fryer basket; at 180°C/350°F, cook for 20 minutes, basting and turning occasionally, or until cooked through.
4 Serve chicken brushed with extra barbecue sauce.

match it Fetta, Dill & Bacon Potatoes, page 195.

prep + cook time 30 minutes
serves 4

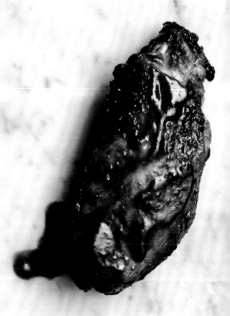

PICK-A-FLAVOUR
PIZZA NIGHT

2 x 250g (8oz) fresh dough balls
(see tip)
⅔ cup (170g) tomato pasta sauce
1 medium red onion (170g),
sliced thinly
4 centre-cut bacon rashers (140g),
sliced
100g (3oz) pancetta, torn
1 cured chorizo (170g), sliced
300g (9½oz) mozzarella, sliced
1 small red chilli, sliced
to serve: basil leaves

1 Preheat a 5.3-litre air fryer to 180°C/350°F for 3 minutes.
2 Join dough balls into one large ball on a lightly floured surface. Roll out into a 16cm x 26cm (6½in x 10½in) oval on a piece of baking paper. Trim baking paper so it is 3cm (1¼in) larger all around than the dough base.
3 Spread base with pasta sauce; top with onion, bacon, pancetta, chorizo, mozzarella and chilli (or choose another pizza flavour).
4 Taking care, using the paper as an aid, lower the pizza into the air fryer basket. Reset the temperature to 170°C/340°F; cook for 15 minutes until pizza crust is golden and cooked through.
5 Serve pizza topped with basil leaves.

other flavours

prawn Omit the meats and mozzarella and replace with 8 uncooked peeled, cleaned prawns tossed in 2 teaspoons extra virgin olive oil. Serve topped with rocket and grated lemon rind.
gimme greens Omit the meats and replace with 175g (5½oz) halved broccolini stalks and ¼ cup halved kalamata olives. Serve topped with crumbled goat's cheese and grated lemon rind.
eggplant & ricotta Omit the meats and replace with 450g (14½oz) chargrilled eggplant slices and 100g (3oz) ricotta. Serve topped with pesto.

tip You can find fresh dough balls in the refrigerated section of the supermarket.

prep + cook time 25 minutes
makes 1 pizza (serves 2)

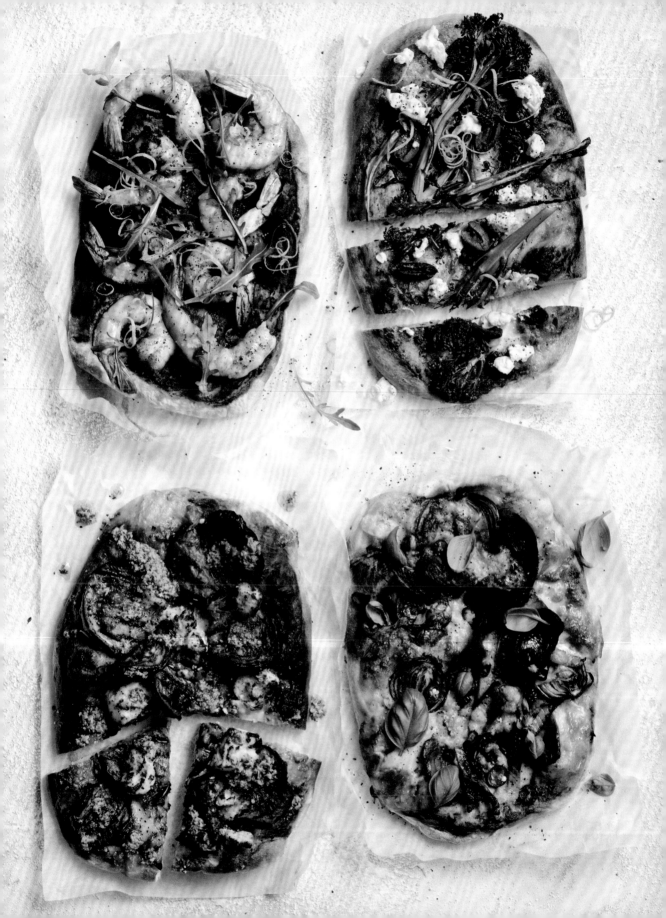

SOY & SRIRACHA GLAZED CHICKEN

2 tbsp soy sauce

1 tsp sriracha chilli sauce

2 tbsp maple syrup

1 tbsp sesame seeds, toasted

8 chicken thigh fillets (1.3kg)

2 bunches baby pak choy,
   halved lengthways

400g (12½oz) packet microwave
   jasmine rice

3 green onions (scallions), sliced thinly

1 Combine sauces, maple syrup and half the sesame seeds in a shallow bowl; add chicken and turn to coat.

2 Line the base of the pan of a 7-litre air fryer with foil. Preheat to 200°C/400°F for 3 minutes.

3 Taking care, place chicken in the air fryer basket, reserving the marinade; at 200°C/400°F, cook for 20 minutes, turning and basting with the reserved marinade halfway through the cooking time, until cooked through. When chicken has 3 minutes left, top with pak choy, cut-side up.

4 Meanwhile, reheat rice following packet directions; transfer to a medium bowl and stir in three-quarters of the green onion.

5 Serve chicken with rice and pak choy, topped with remaining green onion and sesame seeds.

prep + cook time 30 minutes
serves 4

SALMON
FISH CAKES

3 medium floury potatoes (600g), chopped coarsely
2 tbsp olive oil
olive oil cooking spray
400g (12½oz) skinless boneless salmon fillets
2 green onions (scallions), sliced thinly
2 tsp finely grated lemon rind
1 tbsp finely chopped dill or parsley
1 egg, beaten lightly
1½ cups (110g) panko (japanese) breadcrumbs
Pick-a-sauce (see page 100)
to serve: lime wedges

1 Preheat a 5.3-litre air fryer to 180°C/350°F for 3 minutes.

2 Boil, steam or microwave potatoes until tender; drain. Mash potatoes with olive oil until smooth.

3 Meanwhile, spray the air fryer basket with oil. Taking care, place salmon in the basket; at 180°C/350°F, cook for 6 minutes until salmon is cooked through. Pull out the air fryer pan and basket; cool salmon in the basket.

4 Flake salmon into the mashed potato; mash until salmon breaks into smaller pieces. Add green onion, lemon rind, dill, egg and half the breadcrumbs, then season; stir to combine. With damp hands, shape mixture into eight patties; place on a tray. Freeze for 10 minutes to firm.

5 Coat patties in remaining breadcrumbs; spray generously with oil.

6 Place patties in the air fryer basket; at 180°C/350°F, cook for 8 minutes, turning halfway through cooking time, or until golden and heated through.

7 Serve fish cakes with your choice of Pick-a-sauce and lime wedges.

swap it To make red curry fish cakes, use the equivalent weight of sweet potatoes instead of floury potatoes and stir 2 tablespoons thai red curry paste into the mash; use coriander (cilantro) instead of dill.

prep + cook time 45 minutes (+ cooling & freezing)
makes 8

TIP Short on time? Use a 475g (15oz) tub of mashed potato (or sweet potato) and 300g (9½oz) hot-smoked trout.

CHICKEN WINGS

prep + cook time 50 minutes (+ refrigeration) **serves** 4

Toss 1.5kg (3lb) chicken wings with chosen marinade opposite in a
large bowl. Refrigerate for 1–2 hours. Preheat air fryer to 180°C/350°F
for 3 minutes. Taking care, place chicken in the air fryer basket;
cook for 40 minutes, turning occasionally, until chicken is cooked.

sticky sesame

pineapple
huli huli

smoky
barbecue

sticky pomegranate

STICKY SESAME

Combine 4 thinly sliced green onions (scallions), 3 crushed cloves garlic, ¼ cup each soy sauce and chinese cooking wine (shao hsing), 3 tsp finely grated ginger and 2 tbsp brown sugar in a bowl. Serve cooked wings topped with 2 tbsp toasted sesame seeds and extra sliced green onion.

PINEAPPLE HULI HULI

Combine ⅓ cup firmly packed brown sugar, ⅔ cup fresh pineapple juice, ½ cup each tomato sauce (ketchup) and soy sauce, ⅓ cup malt vinegar, 1 tbsp finely grated ginger and 2 crushed cloves garlic in a frying pan. Boil over medium heat for 5 minutes. Sprinkle wings with 1 tbsp paprika before tossing in marinade. Serve cooked wings topped with coriander (cilantro).

CHICKEN WINGS

4 WAYS

STICKY POMEGRANATE

Stir 1 cup firmly packed brown sugar, 1½ cups pomegranate juice, 3 tsp grated orange rind, 2 crushed cloves garlic, 1½ tbsp each dijon mustard and worcestershire sauce, and ⅓ cup tomato sauce (ketchup) in a saucepan. Bring to the boil; stir occasionally over medium heat for 10 minutes or until reduced by half. Serve cooked wings topped with pomegranate seeds.

SMOKY BARBECUE

Combine ½ cup honey, ½ cup smoky barbecue sauce and 2 tbsp teriyaki sauce in a bowl. Serve cooked wings with thinly sliced long red chilli and lime wedges.

STUFFED EGGPLANT WITH LENTILS

2 large eggplants (1kg),
    halved lengthways
2 tsp table salt
olive oil cooking spray
1 tbsp extra virgin olive oil
1 medium onion (150g), chopped finely
2 cloves garlic, crushed
1 tsp ground cumin
1 tsp smoked paprika
400g (12½oz) can brown lentils,
    drained, rinsed
400g (12½oz) can cherry tomatoes
¼ cup chopped oregano leaves
100g (3oz) fetta, crumbled
⅓ cup (25g) finely grated parmesan
to serve: extra oregano leaves

1 Using a small, sharp knife, score the cut side of eggplant halves in a diamond pattern without cutting all the way through; season with salt. Place, cut-side down, on a wire rack for 30 minutes; rinse and pat dry with paper towel. Using a teaspoon, scoop out eggplant flesh, leaving a 1cm (½in) thick shell. Finely chop eggplant flesh. Spray eggplant shells with oil.

2 Preheat a 7-litre air fryer to 180°C/350°F for 3 minutes.

3 Taking care, place eggplant shells, cut-side up, in the air fryer basket; at 180°C/350°F, cook for 12 minutes until softened.

4 Meanwhile, heat oil in a large frying pan over medium-high heat; cook onion, stirring, for 5 minutes or until softened. Add garlic, cumin and paprika; cook, stirring, for 1 minute or until fragrant. Add eggplant flesh; cook, stirring occasionally, for 5 minutes or until tender. Add lentils and tomatoes; bring to a simmer. Stir in oregano; season. Cool for 5 minutes. Stir half the fetta into the lentil mixture.

5 Transfer eggplant shells to a plate. Spoon lentil mixture into the shells, then sprinkle with parmesan and remaining fetta; spray lightly with oil.

6 Taking care, place stuffed eggplants in the air fryer basket; at 180°C/350°F, cook for 8 minutes until lightly browned and tender.

7 Serve stuffed eggplants scattered with extra oregano leaves.

prep + cook time 50 minutes (+ standing)
serves 4

MOZZARELLA MUSHROOM BURGER

8 portobello mushrooms (400g)
1 tbsp balsamic vinegar
1 tbsp extra virgin olive oil
4 large brioche buns (400g), split
¼ cup (75g) aïoli
40g (1½oz) mixed salad leaves
1 large tomato (220g), sliced
125g (4oz) fresh mozzarella ball,
    cut into 4 slices
⅓ cup (90g) basil pesto
to serve: shoestring fries and low-sugar
    tomato sauce (ketchup)

1 Place mushrooms, vinegar and oil in a medium bowl, then season; toss to coat.

2 Preheat a 7-litre air fryer to 180°C/350°F for 3 minutes.

3 Taking care, place the mushrooms in the air fryer basket; at 180°C/350°F, cook for 12 minutes, turning halfway through cooking time, until tender.

4 Spread bun bases with aïoli, then top with salad leaves, tomato, mozzarella, mushrooms and pesto; sandwich together with bun tops.

5 Serve mushroom burgers with shoestring fries and tomato sauce.

prep + cook time 25 minutes
serves 4

CHICKEN CHIMICHANGAS WITH AVOCADO SALSA

3 cups (480g) shredded cooked chicken
30g (1oz) packet taco seasoning
1 cup (120g) coarsely grated cheddar
200g (6½oz) jar taco sauce
4 x 20cm (8in) flour tortillas,
   warmed slightly
olive oil cooking spray
1 medium avocado (250g), diced
1 medium tomato (150g), chopped
½ small red onion (50g), chopped finely
2 tbsp finely chopped coriander
   (cilantro)
1 tbsp lime juice
1 tbsp extra virgin olive oil
2 baby gem lettuce, torn

1 Combine chicken, taco seasoning, cheddar and ⅓ cup taco sauce in a bowl; season. Divide chicken mixture among tortillas, placing along the centre of each one; flatten chicken mixture slightly and shape into a rectangle. Fold in ends of tortillas, then roll up to enclose the filling; spray all over with oil.

2 Preheat a 7-litre air fryer to 180°C/350°F for 3 minutes.

3 Taking care, place chimichangas, seam-side down, in the air fryer basket; at 180°C/350°F, cook for 12 minutes, turning halfway through cooking time, until golden and filling is hot.

4 Meanwhile, to make avocado salsa, combine avocado, tomato, onion, coriander, lime juice and oil in a bowl; season.

5 To serve, divide the chimichangas, lettuce and avocado salsa among plates; drizzle chimichangas with remaining taco sauce.

prep + cook time 45 minutes
serves 4

CRISP SKINNED SALMON
WITH SALSA VERDE

---

4 x 185g (6oz) salmon fillets, skin on
1 tbsp extra virgin olive oil
2 tsp sea salt flakes
1 small shallot (eschalot),
　chopped finely
1 clove garlic, crushed
2 tsp finely grated lemon rind
2 tbsp lemon juice
2 tbsp finely chopped dill
¼ cup chopped flat-leaf parsley
2 tbsp chopped chives
1 tbsp baby capers, chopped coarsely
to serve: extra sea salt flakes

1 Preheat a 7-litre air fryer to 200°C/400°F for 3 minutes.
2 Rub salmon with oil, then sprinkle with salt flakes.
3 Taking care, line the air fryer basket with a silicone mat, if available (see page 11). Place salmon, skin-side up, in the basket; at 200°C/400°F, cook for 8 minutes until skin is crisp and salmon is cooked to your liking.
4 Meanwhile, to make salsa verde, combine remaining ingredients in a medium bowl, then season; mix well.
5 Serve salmon topped with salsa verde and sprinkled with extra salt flakes.

match it Mustard & Mint Potatoes, page 195.

prep + cook time 25 minutes
serves 4

PEPPERONI
CALZONES

200g (6½oz) piece pepperoni,
    sliced thinly
1 medium red capsicum (bell pepper)
    (200g), sliced thinly
250g (8oz) frozen chopped spinach,
    thawed
⅓ cup (50g) semi-dried tomato strips,
    without oil
2 tbsp chopped oregano
⅔ cup (70g) coarsely grated mozzarella
2 x 250g (8oz) fresh dough balls
¼ cup (65g) thick pizza sauce
    (tomato paste with herbs)
to serve: sea salt flakes

1 Heat a large non-stick frying pan over medium-high heat; cook pepperoni and capsicum, stirring, for 5 minutes or until golden and tender. Transfer to a plate lined with paper towel to cool.

2 Meanwhile, squeeze spinach to remove excess liquid; transfer to a medium bowl. Add pepperoni mixture, semi-dried tomatoes, oregano and mozzarella; stir to combine.

3 Divide each dough ball into two even pieces. Roll dough portions out on a piece of lightly floured baking paper into 18cm (7¼in) rounds. Spread dough rounds evenly with pizza sauce, leaving a 1.5cm (¾in) border around the edge. Top half of each dough round with pepperoni filling mixture, then fold dough over to enclose filling; pinch edges to seal, then fold edges over themselves to pleat. Using a small, sharp knife, make three cuts in the tops. Trim the baking paper so it is 3cm (1¼in) larger all around than two of the calzones together.

4 Preheat a 7-litre air fryer to 180°C/350°F for 3 minutes.

5 Taking care, using the paper as an aid, lower the two calzones into the air fryer basket; at 180°C/350°F, cook for 14 minutes, turning halfway through cooking time, or until crust is golden and calzones are cooked through. Transfer to a plate; cover to keep warm. Repeat cooking with remaining calzones.

6 Sprinkle calzones with salt flakes to serve.

prep + cook time 45 minutes
serves 4

SALT & PEPPER SQUID

1kg (2lb) small whole squid or
  600g (1¼lb) cleaned squid
1½ tbsp salt flakes, crushed lightly
2 tsp coarsely ground black pepper
3 tsp ground sichuan pepper
1 tsp chilli powder
⅔ cup (100g) cornflour (cornstarch)
½ tsp baking powder
1 cup (250ml) milk
cooking oil spray
4 long red chillies, seeded, sliced thinly
1 green onion (scallion), sliced thinly
2 medium lemons (280g), halved
  or cut into wedges

1 If using a whole squid, clean by pulling the head and tentacles away from the body. Pull out the clear backbone and remove the entrails. Cut tentacles away from head just below the eyes; discard head. Discard hard beak in the centre of tentacles. Cut tentacles in half, or quarters if large. Remove side wings and rub membrane from the body. Rinse body, tentacles and wings thoroughly. Cut the squid hoods down one side; open out and pat dry. Score the inside lightly with a small, sharp knife in a criss-cross pattern without cutting all the way through. Cut squid hoods into 2.5cm x 5cm (1in x 2in) pieces. Pat squid dry with paper towel.

2 Preheat a 5.3-litre air fryer to 200°C/400°F for 3 minutes.

3 Meanwhile, combine salt flakes, peppers and chilli powder in a medium bowl; reserve 2 teaspoons spice mix to serve. Sift cornflour and baking powder over remaining spice mix. Stir squid in milk; drain. Toss squid in flour mixture to coat, shaking off excess; spray generously with oil.

4 Spray the air fryer basket with oil. Taking care, place half the squid in the basket; at 200°C/400°F, cook for 6 minutes, turning halfway through cooking time, or until golden and cooked through. Transfer to a tray; cover to keep warm. Repeat cooking with remaining squid and oil spray, adding sliced chilli and green onion during the last 30 seconds of cooking time.

5 Top squid with sliced chilli and green onion; sprinkle with the reserved spice mix. Serve with lemon halves.

prep + cook time 30 minutes
serves 4

PICK-A-SAUCE

GREEN OLIVE DRESSING

prep time 5 minutes **makes** ¾ cup

Process ½ cup pitted green sicilian olives, 2 tbsp oregano leaves and ⅓ cup olive oil until almost smooth; season to taste.

FETTA DRESSING

prep time 5 minutes **makes** 1 cup

Process ½ cup greek yoghurt, 100g (3oz) crumbled fetta and 2 tbsp lime juice until smooth; season to taste. Stir in 1 tsp finely grated lime rind.

MISO AVOCADO DRESSING

prep time 5 minutes **makes** ¾ cup

Process 1 chopped medium avocado (250g), 3 tsp white (shiro) miso and ¼ cup (75g) mayonnaise until smooth; season to taste.

CHILLI & LIME MAYO

prep time 5 minutes **makes** about 1½ cups

Combine 1 cup mayonnaise with ¼ cup sriracha chilli sauce and
2 tbsp lime juice in a small bowl.

CHILLI PEANUT DRESSING

prep time 10 minutes **makes** ¾ cup

Process 1 clove crushed garlic, 1 finely chopped long red chilli,
⅓ cup roasted unsalted peanuts, ¼ cup fresh lime juice, the roots
from 1 bunch coriander (cilantro), 2 tbsp brown sugar, 1 tbsp
soy sauce and 1 tbsp water until peanuts are finely chopped and
ingredients are combined.

CHIMICHURRI

prep time 5 minutes **makes** 1¼ cups

Blend or process 2 tbsp red wine vinegar, ½ cup extra virgin
olive oil, 4 cloves finely chopped garlic, ½ tsp dried chilli flakes,
1 tsp salt flakes, 2 cups flat-leaf parsley leaves and 2 tbsp oregano
leaves until finely chopped.

ITALIAN CHICKEN RISSOLES

500g (1lb) minced (ground) chicken
1 egg
2 tbsp pine nuts, toasted lightly
¼ cup finely chopped basil
1 clove garlic, crushed
60g (2oz) semi-dried tomatoes, chopped
1 cup (75g) panko (japanese) breadcrumbs
8 thin slices prosciutto (60g), halved lengthways
olive oil cooking spray
1 bunch rocket (arugula), trimmed
1 tbsp extra virgin olive oil
1 tbsp balsamic vinegar
2 tbsp shaved parmesan

1 Combine chicken, egg, pine nuts, basil, garlic, semi-dried tomatoes and half the breadcrumbs in a medium bowl, then season; mix well. Shape mixture into eight 2cm-thick rissoles. Roll rissoles in remaining breadcrumbs to coat lightly. Wrap one strip of prosciutto around each rissole, then another to make a cross shape, twisting ends to secure; lightly spray all over with oil.

2 Preheat a 7-litre air fryer to 180°C/350°F for 3 minutes.

3 Spray the air fryer basket with oil. Taking care, place the rissoles in the basket; at 180°C/350°F, cook for 8 minutes, turning halfway through cooking time, or until browned and cooked through.

4 Meanwhile, place rocket, oil, vinegar and parmesan in a medium bowl; toss gently to combine.

5 Serve rissoles with rocket salad.

prep + cook time 30 minutes
serves 4

SPICED PRAWN PO-BOYS

2 eggs

¼ cup (55g) panko (japanese)
   breadcrumbs

1 tbsp cajun seasoning

16 uncooked prawns (shrimp),
   peeled, deveined

olive oil cooking spray

1 long baguette

⅓ cup (100g) mayonnaise

1 baby cos (romaine) lettuce (180g),
   leaves separated

2 medium tomatoes (300g),
   sliced thinly

3 gherkins, cut into rounds

to serve: extra mayonnaise, chopped
   chives and extra gherkins

1 Lightly beat eggs and 1 tablespoon water in a shallow bowl. Combine breadcrumbs and cajun seasoning in a second shallow bowl. Dip prawns in egg, then coat in breadcrumb mixture; spray generously all over with oil.

2 Preheat a 7-litre air fryer to 180°C/350°F for 3 minutes.

3 Taking care, place prawns in the air fryer basket in a single layer; at 180°C/350°F, cook for 6 minutes, turning halfway through cooking time, until golden brown and cooked through.

4 Trim ends from baguette and discard; cut into four even pieces, then split horizontally, being careful not to cut all the way through. Spread bases with mayonnaise, then fill with lettuce, tomato, gherkins and prawns; drizzle with extra mayonnaise and sprinkle with chopped chives. Serve with extra gherkins.

prep + cook time 35 minutes
serves 4

CLASSIC
MEATBALLS

2 slices white bread (90g)
⅓ cup (80ml) milk
1 medium onion (150g), grated coarsely
2 cloves garlic, crushed
1 medium carrot (120g), grated finely
750g (1½lb) minced (ground) beef
¼ cup chopped flat-leaf parsley
1 egg, beaten lightly
2 tbsp tomato paste
olive oil cooking spray
1½ cups (420g) tomato passata
400g (12½oz) jar olive pasta sauce
to serve: lasagnette (or spaghetti),
    grated parmesan and basil leaves

1 Tear bread into a large bowl; pour over milk. Add onion, garlic, carrot, beef, parsley, egg and tomato paste; season well. Stand for 10 minutes without stirring.

2 Preheat a 5.3-litre air fryer to 200°C/400°F for 5 minutes.

3 Using your hands, combine ingredients well in the bowl. With damp hands, shape 1½ tablespoons of mince mixture into balls; spray with oil.

4 Spray the air fryer basket with oil. Taking care, place half the meatballs in the basket in a single layer; at 200°C/400°F, cook for 10 minutes, shaking basket halfway through cooking time, until browned and cooked through. Transfer to a tray; cover to keep warm. Repeat cooking with remaining meatballs.

5 Combine passata and pasta sauce in a bowl. Roll meatballs in tomato sauce mixture; place in a 15cm x 22cm (6in x 8¾in), 1.5-litre (6-cup) oval heatproof dish.

Pour remaining tomato sauce mixture over meatballs. Place dish in the basket; at 200°C/400°F, cook for 10 minutes until heated through.

6 Serve lasagnette topped with meatballs and sauce, grated parmesan and basil leaves.

other flavours

greek lamb meatballs Swap beef mince for lamb mince and parsley for oregano. Add 2 teaspoons ground cinnamon and ½ teaspoon chilli flakes to tomato sauce mixture in step 5. Serve with orzo (risoni), greek yoghurt and pine nuts.

mexican stuffed meatballs Add 2 teaspoons ground cumin and 1 teaspoon Tabasco chipotle sauce to meatball mixture in step 1. Combine 150g (4½oz) each grated mozzarella and cheddar; roll into small balls and press into the centre of each meatball in step 3.

prep + cook time 45 minutes
serves 6

PREP IT The chicken can be prepared to the end of step 2 up to 4 hours ahead; refrigerate until required.

CRUMBED
CHICKEN WITH
SPICY
MAYO

½ cup (75g) plain (all-purpose) flour
2 eggs
1 cup (75g) panko (japanese)
   breadcrumbs
½ cup (40g) finely grated parmesan
¼ cup coarsely chopped flat-leaf parsley
2 tsp finely grated lemon rind
12 chicken tenderloins (900g)
olive oil cooking spray
3 cups (75g) mixed salad leaves
2 tsp lemon juice
to serve: lemon wedges

SPICY MAYONNAISE
⅔ cup (200g) mayonnaise
¾ tsp piri piri seasoning
2 tsp lemon juice

1 Preheat a 5.3-litre air fryer to 180°C/350°F for 3 minutes.
2 Place flour in a shallow bowl; season with salt and freshly ground black pepper. Lightly beat eggs in a second shallow bowl. Combine breadcrumbs, parmesan, parsley and lemon rind in a third shallow bowl. Dust chicken in flour, shaking off excess, dip in egg, then coat in breadcrumb mixture; spray generously with oil.
3 Taking care, place chicken in the air fryer basket; at 180°C/350°F, cook for 8 minutes, turning halfway through cooking time, or until golden and cooked through.
4 Meanwhile, to make spicy mayonnaise, combine ingredients in a small bowl.
5 Place salad leaves in a medium bowl with lemon juice; toss to combine.
6 Serve crumbed chicken with spicy mayonnaise, salad leaves and lemon wedges.

prep + cook time 25 minutes
serves 4

109

LEMON
& GARLIC
ROAST CHICKEN

60g (2oz) butter, softened
1 clove garlic, crushed
1 tsp sweet paprika
2 tsp chopped rosemary
1 tsp chopped thyme
1.2kg (2½lb) whole chicken
½ medium lemon (70g), halved
8 sprigs lemon thyme
cooking oil spray
1 bulb garlic, halved
4 sprigs bay leaves
1 cup (250ml) gravy

1 Preheat a 5.3-litre air fryer to 160°C/325°F for 3 minutes.
2 Combine butter, garlic, paprika, rosemary and thyme in a small bowl.
3 Remove and discard any fat from cavity of chicken. Pat the cavity and skin dry with paper towel. Tuck wings under body. Run your fingers carefully between the skin and the breast meat. Push butter mixture under skin to cover breast. Fill cavity of chicken with lemon and half the thyme sprigs. Tie legs together with kitchen string.
4 Spray the air fryer basket with oil. Taking care, place chicken in the basket and cover loosely with foil; at 160°C/325°F, cook for 30 minutes.

5 Uncover chicken and place garlic bulb halves and bay leaves beside it; at 160°C/325°F, cook for a further 30 minutes until juices run clear when a skewer is inserted into the thickest part of a thigh. Transfer chicken, garlic and bay leaves to a dish; stand for 10 minutes.
6 Serve chicken with the bay leaves, garlic, remaining thyme sprigs and warm gravy.

prep + cook time 1¼ hours
serves 4

PREP IT Patties can be prepared a day ahead; refrigerate until required. Brush with barbecue sauce before cooking.

LOADED KOREAN BURGER
WITH KIMCHI SLAW

1 tbsp brown sugar
2 tbsp soy sauce
¼ cup (85g) gochujang chilli paste
   (see tips)
2 cloves garlic, crushed
2 tsp finely grated ginger
700g (1½lb) minced (ground) beef
1 egg
¾ cup (75g) packaged breadcrumbs
2 tbsp barbecue sauce
cooking oil spray
4 slices cheddar (160g)
4 large brioche buns (400g)
⅓ cup (100g) japanese mayonnaise
to serve: sweet potato chips

KIMCHI SLAW
¼ cup (25g) kimchi, shredded finely
2 tsp rice wine vinegar
2 tsp vegetable oil
2 tsp sesame oil
2 cups (160g) shredded cabbage
   (see tips)
⅓ cup mint leaves

1 Preheat a 5.3-litre air fryer to 180°C/350°F for 3 minutes.

2 Combine sugar, soy sauce, all but 1 teaspoon chilli paste, the garlic and ginger in a bowl. Add beef, egg and breadcrumbs; using your hands, combine well. Shape mixture into four patties the same size as the brioche buns; ensure they will all fit in the air fryer basket. Brush all over with barbecue sauce.

3 Spray the air fryer basket with oil. Taking care, place patties in the basket; at 180°C/350°F, cook for 6 minutes, turning halfway through cooking time, or until browned and cooked through. Top each with a slice of cheddar. Slide air fryer pan and basket back into appliance. With air fryer turned off, leave patties for 1 minute for cheddar to melt.

4 Meanwhile, to make kimchi slaw, combine kimchi, vinegar and oils in a large bowl. Add cabbage and mint to bowl; toss to combine.

5 Split and toast brioche buns. Spread bases with combined mayonnaise and remaining chilli paste, then top with patties and slaw; sandwich together with bun tops.

6 Serve burgers with sweet potato chips.

tips Gochujang is a Korean fermented red chilli paste, available in major supermarkets and Asian food stores. Substitute with your favourite chilli sauce, if you prefer, adjusting the amount to your heat tolerance and palate. We used a mix of shredded red cabbage and wombok (napa cabbage); however, you can use any cabbage mix you like, including coleslaw mixes.

prep + cook time 30 minutes
makes 4

PORTUGUESE CHICKEN DRUMSTICKS

2 cloves garlic, chopped
1 long red chilli, chopped
1 tbsp finely chopped oregano
2 tbsp apple cider vinegar
1 tbsp extra virgin olive oil
1 tbsp brown sugar
2 tsp smoked paprika
1 tsp sea salt flakes
8 chicken drumsticks (1.2kg)

1 To make marinade, place garlic, chilli and oregano in a small food processor or blender; blend until finely chopped. Add vinegar, oil, sugar, paprika and salt; process until combined.
2 Place chicken in a large shallow dish; add marinade and toss to coat. Cover with plastic wrap. Refrigerate for 2 hours.
3 Preheat a 7-litre air fryer to 200°C/400°F for 3 minutes.

4 Taking care, place drained chicken in the air fryer basket; at 200°C/400°F, cook for 25 minutes, turning halfway through cooking time, or until cooked through.

tip Heat drained marinade in a small saucepan for 3 minutes until reduced and thickened slightly, then use to baste the chicken while cooking.

prep + cook time 40 minutes (+ refrigeration)
serves 4

TIP For extra flavoursome nuggets, dissolve 2 tablespoons salt in 2 cups cold water, then add the chicken. Refrigerate for 1¼ hours; drain. Continue with the recipe.

GLUTEN-FREE
CHICKEN
NUGGETS

2 x 300g (9½oz) chicken breast fillets

2 cups (80g) cornflakes

⅔ cup (105g) gluten-free plain
   (all-purpose) flour

2 tsp ground paprika

1 tsp onion salt

⅓ cup (25g) finely grated parmesan

2 eggs

olive oil cooking spray

2 tsp sriracha chilli sauce

⅔ cup (150g) aïoli

to serve: basil leaves and lemon wedges

1 Preheat a 5.3-litre air fryer to 180°C/350°F for 3 minutes.

2 Cut chicken into nugget-sized pieces. Crush the cornflakes by hand in a medium bowl until coarsely crushed. Add ⅓ cup (50g) of the flour, the paprika, onion salt and parmesan; season with salt and freshly ground black pepper. Lightly beat eggs in another medium bowl. Place remaining flour in a third medium bowl. Dust a few of the chicken pieces at a time in flour, shaking off excess, dip into egg, then coat in the spiced cornflake mixture; spray generously with oil.

3 Taking care, place half the nuggets in the basket; at 180°C/350°F, cook for 8 minutes, turning halfway through cooking time, or until golden and cooked through. Transfer to a platter; cover to keep warm. Repeat cooking with remaining nuggets.

4 Swirl sriracha through aïoli. Serve chicken nuggets with basil leaves, lemon wedges and aïoli.

prep + cook time 35 minutes
serves 4

VEGIES & SIDES

The air fryer can make your side dishes the stars of the meal. Think warm veg salads, jacket potatoes, loaded corn, mac 'n' cheese croquettes, salt 'n' pepper tofu, popcorn cauliflower and more.

CAJUN
SWEET POTATO
WEDGES

2 tsp ground cumin
1 tsp ground coriander
1 tsp garlic salt
½ tsp smoked paprika
½ tsp dried thyme
½ tsp dried oregano
½ tsp cayenne pepper
1kg (2lb) small sweet potatoes
1 tbsp extra virgin olive oil
to serve: sea salt flakes, chopped
    coriander (cilantro) and sour cream

1 Preheat a 7-litre air fryer to 200°C/400°F for 3 minutes.

2 To make cajun spice mix, combine cumin, coriander, garlic salt, paprika, thyme, oregano and cayenne pepper in a small bowl.

3 Scrub sweet potatoes and pat dry; cut into long thin wedges. Place in a large bowl with oil and the cajun spice mix; toss to coat.

4 Taking care, place wedges in the air fryer basket; at 200°C/400°F, cook for 15 minutes, turning halfway through cooking time, or until golden and cooked through.

5 Sprinkle wedges with salt flakes and chopped coriander. Serve with sour cream.

prep + cook time 25 minutes
serves 4

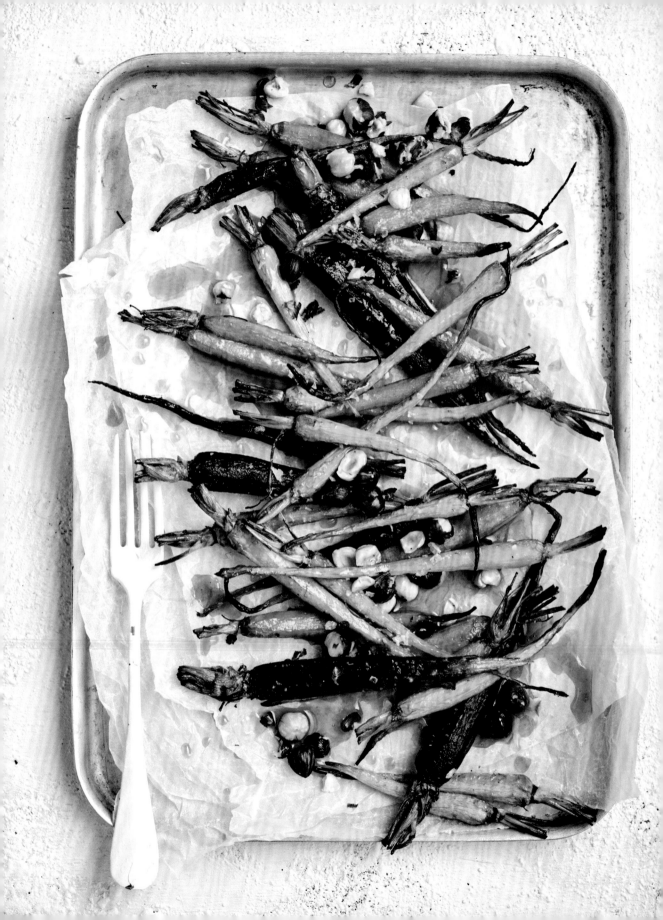

MAPLE-ROASTED CARROTS WITH HAZELNUTS

2 bunches baby (dutch) mixed colour
    carrots (500g), peeled
20g (¾oz) butter, melted
1 tbsp extra virgin olive oil
2 tbsp maple syrup
1 clove garlic, crushed
¼ cup (35g) unroasted hazelnuts

1 Preheat a 7-litre air fryer to 200°C/400°F for 3 minutes.

2 Cut any large carrots in half lengthways. Place carrots in a large bowl with butter, oil, maple syrup and garlic, then season; toss to combine.

3 Taking care, place carrots in the air fryer basket, reserving any leftover butter mixture in the bowl; at 200°C/400°F, cook for 10 minutes, turning halfway through cooking time.

4 Scatter hazelnuts over carrots; at 200°C/400°F, cook for a further 5 minutes or until carrots are golden and tender.

5 To serve, drizzle carrots and hazelnuts with reserved butter mixture.

prep + cook time 25 minutes
serves 4

HOT & SPICY POPCORN CAULIFLOWER

2 tbsp linseed (flaxseed) meal
¼ cup (70g) dijon mustard
2 tbsp hot sauce (see tip)
1⅔ cups (250g) plain (all-purpose) flour
2 tsp onion powder
2 tsp garlic powder
2 tsp smoked paprika
½ tsp cayenne pepper
½ tsp ground white pepper
1 medium cauliflower (1.5kg)
olive oil cooking spray
to serve: hot sauce and lemon wedges

1 Combine linseed meal with ⅔ cup (160ml) water in a large bowl; stand for 5 minutes or until thickened. Add mustard and hot sauce; stir to combine. Combine flour, onion powder, garlic powder and spices in another large bowl; season with salt.
2 Cut the cauliflower into 2.5cm (1in) florets.
3 Preheat a 5.3-litre air fryer to 180°C/350°F for 3 minutes.
4 Add cauliflower to linseed mixture; stir to coat. Working in batches, toss cauliflower in flour mixture to coat; spray generously with oil.

5 Taking care, place half the cauliflower in the air fryer basket; at 180°C/350°F, cook for 10 minutes until golden. Transfer to a bowl; season with salt and cover to keep warm. Repeat cooking with remaining cauliflower.
6 Serve popcorn cauliflower with hot sauce and lemon wedges.

serve it You can also serve the popcorn cauliflower with a 400g (12½oz) jar of your favourite pasta sauce, heated up.

prep + cook time 40 minutes
serves 4

TIP Use whatever hot sauce you have on hand, such as a sriracha or mexican hot sauce.

SALT & PEPPER TOFU

450g (14½oz) packet firm tofu
2 egg whites
¼ cup (35g) cornflour (cornstarch)
¼ cup (45g) rice flour
1 tbsp sea salt flakes
1 tbsp mixed peppercorns,
    freshly ground
olive oil cooking spray
1 large carrot (180g), julienned
1 telegraph cucumber (400g),
    seeded, julienned
1 medium red capsicum (bell pepper)
    (200g), julienned
2 cups (160g) bean sprouts, trimmed
½ cup coriander (cilantro) leaves
2 tbsp sweet chilli sauce
2 tbsp lime juice
2 tsp sesame oil
1 clove garlic, crushed

1 Cut tofu into 3cm (1¼in) cubes. Line a chopping board with paper towel and place tofu pieces on top. Lay more paper towel on top of tofu, then top with a heavy tray (or small chopping board) to weigh tofu down; leave for 10 minutes to drain.
2 Beat egg whites in a shallow bowl. Combine flours, salt flakes and peppercorns in a second shallow bowl. Dip tofu pieces in egg white, then coat in flour mixture; spray generously all over with oil.
3 Preheat a 7-litre air fryer to 200°C/400°F for 3 minutes.
4 Taking care, place tofu in the air fryer basket; at 200°C/400°F, cook for 10 minutes, turning halfway through cooking time, or until crisp and golden.

5 Meanwhile, combine carrot, cucumber, capsicum, sprouts and coriander in a medium bowl. Whisk sweet chilli sauce, lime juice, sesame oil and garlic in a small bowl. Add dressing to salad; toss to combine.
6 To serve, divide salad and tofu among plates.

prep + cook time 35 minutes (+ standing)
serves 4

127

AVOCADO FRIES WITH LIME
DIPPING SAUCE

2 medium slightly under-ripe avocados
    (300g), halved, pitted, peeled
2 eggs
½ cup (35g) panko (japanese)
    breadcrumbs
½ cup (40g) finely grated parmesan
olive oil cooking spray
¾ cup (200g) greek yoghurt
2 tsp finely grated lime rind
1 tbsp lime juice
to serve: sea salt flakes

1 Preheat a 7-litre air fryer to 180°C/350°F for 3 minutes.

2 Cut each avocado half into five wedges. Lightly beat eggs in a shallow bowl. Combine breadcrumbs and parmesan in a second shallow bowl. Add avocado wedges to egg and toss to coat, then coat in breadcrumb mixture; spray generously all over with oil.

3 Taking care, place avocado fries in the air fryer basket; at 180°C/350°F, cook for 12 minutes, turning halfway through cooking time, or until golden.

4 Meanwhile, to make lime dipping sauce, combine yoghurt, lime rind and juice in a small bowl; season to taste.

5 Sprinkle avocado fries with salt flakes and serve with lime dipping sauce.

prep + cook time 30 minutes
serves 4

SALT 'N' VINEGAR SMASHED POTATOES

1.2kg (2½lb) royal red potatoes,
   halved if large
3 cups (750ml) white vinegar
1 tbsp cooking salt
¼ cup (60ml) extra virgin olive oil
1 bulb garlic, cloves separated
1 bunch rosemary sprigs

1 Place potatoes in a large saucepan. Add vinegar, salt and enough water to just cover; bring to the boil. Boil, partially covered, for 15–20 minutes (the time will vary depending on the size of the potatoes) or until potatoes are tender; drain.

2 Preheat a 5.3-litre air fryer to 200°C/400°F for 3 minutes.

3 Transfer potatoes to a large oven tray. Using a potato masher or the back of a spoon, press down on potatoes until flattened slightly and skins split. Brush potatoes with oil.

4 Taking care, place potatoes in the air fryer basket; at 200°C/400°F, cook for 30 minutes, turning twice during cooking time, or until potatoes are golden. Add garlic 10 minutes into cooking time and rosemary in the last 5 minutes.

5 Season smashed potatoes generously with salt. Serve with roast garlic and rosemary sprigs.

prep + cook time 55 minutes
serves 6

SIDE SALADS

prep time 15 minutes (+ cooling)
serves 4

ITALIAN-STYLE RICE SALAD

Heat a 450g (14½oz) packet microwave brown rice following packet directions; transfer to a large bowl. Add ½ cup (75g) semi-dried tomato strips (not in oil), ⅓ cup basil leaves, 60g (2oz) coarsely chopped baby spinach, ⅔ cup (80g) sliced pitted green sicilian olives, 1 thinly sliced small red onion and ¼ cup (60ml) balsamic dressing. Season to taste. Toss gently to combine.

LENTIL TABBOULEH

Place 2 x 420g (13½oz) cans drained lentils, 1 cup each small flat-leaf parsley and mint leaves, 4 sliced green onions (scallions), 250g (8oz) sliced heirloom cherry tomatoes, ¼ cup (60ml) lemon juice and ¼ cup (60ml) olive oil in a large bowl. Season to taste. Toss gently to combine.

EDAMAME SLAW

Place 2 cups (160g) finely shredded red cabbage, 150g (4½oz) shredded carrot, ½ cup unsalted roasted peanuts, 1 finely chopped long red chilli, 400g (12½oz) peeled and blanched edamame and ½ cup Asian-style sesame, soy and ginger dressing in a large bowl. Season to taste. Toss gently to combine.

KALE, PEAR, SMOKED CHEDDAR & ALMOND SALAD

Place 60g (2oz) chopped kale, 1 medium thinly sliced pear, ⅓ cup (40g) finely grated smoked cheddar, ¼ cup (40g) chopped roasted almond kernels, 2 tbsp lemon juice and 1 tbsp olive oil in a large bowl. Season to taste. Toss gently to combine.

4 WAYS

Italian-style rice salad

lentil tabbouleh

edamame slaw

kale, pear, smoked cheddar & almond salad

BRUSSELS SPROUTS
REVOLUTION

300g (9½oz) broccoli
300g (9½oz) baby red and green
   brussels sprouts
240g (7½oz) kale, stems removed
   and discarded
2 tbsp olive oil
2 tbsp honey
cooking oil spray
2 cloves garlic, sliced thinly
75g (2½oz) prosciutto
⅓ cup (80g) roasted chopped almonds

GREEN TAHINI
2 tbsp tahini
2 tbsp lemon juice
2 tbsp cold water
1 tbsp extra virgin olive oil
⅓ cup baby spinach leaves

1 Preheat a 5.3-litre air fryer to 200°C/400°F for 3 minutes.

2 Cut broccoli into florets. Trim base and remove tough outer leaves from brussels sprouts. Tear leaves from kale into smaller pieces.

3 Combine olive oil and honey in a medium bowl. Add broccoli and brussels sprouts; toss to coat. Season to taste.

4 Taking care, place broccoli mixture in the air fryer basket; at 200°C/400°F, cook for 8 minutes, stirring halfway through cooking time, or until vegetables are beginning to crisp at edges.

5 Place kale leaves in the basket and spray with oil; at 200°C/400°F, cook for 4 minutes.

6 Place garlic and prosciutto on top of vegetables; at 200°C/400°F, cook for 5 minutes until prosciutto is crisp.

7 Meanwhile, to make green tahini, process ingredients until smooth; season to taste. Add a little more water, if necessary, to achieve a drizzling consistency.

8 Serve sprouts mixture with crumbled prosciutto, drizzled with green tahini and topped with almonds.

prep + cook time 35 minutes
serves 4

GOLDEN ONION RINGS

¼ cup (35g) plain (all-purpose) flour
1 tsp smoked paprika
1 egg
1 tbsp cold water
1½ cups (110g) panko (japanese)
    breadcrumbs
2 medium onions (300g), cut into
    1cm (½in) slices, separated into rings
olive oil cooking spray
to serve: aïoli

1 Combine flour and paprika in a shallow bowl; season with salt and freshly ground black pepper. Lightly beat egg and the cold water in a second shallow bowl. Place breadcrumbs in a third shallow bowl. Dust onion rings in flour mixture, shaking off excess, dip in egg, then coat in breadcrumbs; spray generously all over with oil.

2 Preheat a 7-litre air fryer to 190°C/375°F for 3 minutes.

3 Taking care, place half the onion rings in the air fryer basket; at 190°C/375°F, cook for 5 minutes or until golden and tender. Transfer to a wire rack. Repeat cooking with remaining onions rings.

4 Serve onion rings with aïoli.

prep + cook time 25 minutes
serves 4

ROASTED RATATOUILLE

2 zucchini (300g), sliced thickly
1 large red capsicum (bell pepper) (350g), sliced thinly
1 large yellow capsicum (bell pepper) (350g), sliced thinly
1 medium red onion (170g), cut into thin wedges
2 tbsp extra virgin olive oil
1 tsp smoked paprika
250g (8oz) baby roma (egg) tomatoes
2 cloves garlic, sliced thinly
2 tbsp pine nuts
2 tbsp red wine vinegar
½ cup basil leaves

1 Preheat a 7-litre air fryer to 180°C/350°F for 3 minutes.

2 Place zucchini, capsicums, onion, oil and paprika in a large bowl, then season; toss to combine.

3 Taking care, line the air fryer basket with baking paper. Spoon the vegetable mixture onto the paper; at 180°C/350°F, cook for 10 minutes, tossing halfway through cooking time.

4 Add tomatoes, garlic and pine nuts to the basket and toss gently; at 180°C/350°F, cook for a further 5 minutes or until vegetables are browned lightly and tender.

5 Serve ratatouille drizzled with vinegar and topped with basil.

prep + cook time 25 minutes
serves 4

VEGIE MAC 'N' CHEESE CROQUETTES

You will need to start this recipe a day ahead.

1⅓ cups (240g) macaroni
1 medium zucchini (120g), chopped finely
1 cup (140g) frozen peas and corn
50g (1¾oz) butter
1⅓ cups (200g) plain (all-purpose) flour
2 cups (500ml) milk
1 tsp dijon mustard
2 green onions (scallions), sliced thinly
1 small red capsicum (bell pepper) (150g), chopped finely
1 cup (100g) grated pizza cheese
2 eggs
2 cups (150g) panko (japanese) breadcrumbs
¼ cup finely chopped chives
olive oil cooking spray
to serve: sea salt flakes and tomato chutney

1 Grease a 20cm x 30cm (8in x 12in) slice pan; line base and sides with baking paper, extending paper 5cm (2in) over edges.

2 Cook pasta in a large saucepan of boiling salted water following packet directions, adding zucchini and frozen peas and corn for the last 3 minutes of cooking time; drain well. Return pasta and vegetables to pan.

3 Meanwhile, to make cheese sauce, melt butter in a medium saucepan over medium-high heat. Add ⅓ cup (50g) of the flour; cook, stirring, for 2 minutes or until mixture is bubbling. Gradually stir in milk; cook, stirring, for 5 minutes or until sauce boils and thickens. Remove from heat; stir in mustard, green onion, capsicum and cheese until cheese is melted.

4 Pour cheese sauce over pasta and vegetables in pan; stir to combine. Spoon pasta mixture into slice pan; smooth the surface. Refrigerate for 6 hours or overnight until firm.

5 Turn firm pasta mixture onto a clean work surface; cut into 4cm pieces. Place remaining flour in a shallow bowl. Lightly whisk eggs in a second shallow bowl. Combine breadcrumbs and chives in a third shallow bowl. Dust pasta pieces in flour, shaking off excess, dip in egg, then coat in breadcrumb mixture; place on a tray. Refrigerate for 15 minutes.

6 Preheat a 7-litre air fryer to 200°C/400°F for 3 minutes.

7 Spray croquettes generously all over with oil. Taking care, place half the croquettes in the air fryer basket in a single layer; at 200°C/400°F, cook for 10 minutes, turning halfway through cooking time, or until crisp and golden. Using a spatula or egg slide, carefully transfer to a plate; cover loosely with foil to keep warm. Repeat cooking with remaining croquettes.

8 Sprinkle croquettes with salt flakes and serve with tomato chutney.

prep + cook time 50 minutes (+ refrigeration)
serves 4

ROASTED
PUMPKIN WITH
PEPITA
SALSA

1kg (2lb) kent pumpkin, unpeeled,
 cut into 3cm (1¼in) thick wedges
2 tbsp extra virgin olive oil
¼ cup (50g) pepitas (pumpkin seed
 kernels), toasted
250g (8oz) fetta, crumbled
to serve: flat-leaf parsley leaves

PEPITA SALSA
½ cup (100g) pepitas (pumpkin seed
 kernels), toasted
1 cup flat-leaf parsley leaves
½ cup (125ml) extra virgin olive oil
⅓ cup (80ml) lime juice
1 small clove garlic, crushed

1 Preheat a 5.3-litre air fryer to 200°C/400°F for 3 minutes.

2 Place pumpkin and oil in a large bowl; season. Using your fingers, massage the oil onto each pumpkin wedge.

3 Taking care, place pumpkin upright in the air fryer basket; at 200°C/400°F, cook for 40 minutes, turning a number of times during cooking time, until tender.

4 Meanwhile, to make pepita salsa, process ingredients until mixture forms a slightly chunky salsa; season to taste.

5 Serve pumpkin wedges topped with pepita salsa, toasted pepitas, fetta and parsley leaves.

prep it Pepita salsa can be made up to 4 days ahead; refrigerate in a screw-top jar, covered with a thin layer of extra virgin olive oil, until required.

prep + cook time 1 hour
serves 6

DELUXE ROAST VEG

1.2kg (2½lb) baby (chat) potatoes
1 bunch baby orange carrots (250g)
1 bunch baby purple carrots (250g)
1 bunch baby white carrots (525g)
1 whole bulb garlic
1 tbsp fennel seeds
2 tsp smoked paprika
6 bay leaves
2 tbsp extra virgin olive oil

1 Preheat a 5.3-litre air fryer to 200°C/400°F for 3 minutes.
2 Halve potatoes. Trim and scrub unpeeled carrots; cut any larger carrots in half lengthways. Separate unpeeled garlic into cloves. Place potatoes, carrots and garlic in a large bowl with remaining ingredients, then season; toss to combine.
3 Taking care, place the vegetables in the air fryer basket; at 200°C/400°F, cook for 20 minutes, turning halfway through cooking time, or until golden and tender.

swap it You could also use regular carrots, quartered lengthways, in place of baby carrots, if preferred, as well as parsnips, with a few sprigs of rosemary instead of bay leaves.

prep + cook time 30 minutes
serves 4

POTATO
GRATIN

750g (1½lb) potatoes, peeled
⅔ cup (160ml) pouring cream, warmed
⅓ cup (80ml) milk, warmed
2 cloves garlic, crushed
1 tbsp rosemary leaves
1 small onion (80g), sliced thinly
1 cup (120g) grated gruyère cheese
to serve: sea salt flakes

1 Using a mandoline, V-slicer or sharp knife, slice potatoes very thinly.
2 Whisk cream, milk, garlic and rosemary in a large jug until combined; season.
3 Layer potato slices, onion and cream mixture in a 20cm (8in) round ovenproof dish, finishing with the cream mixture. Using your hands, press down firmly on the potatoes.
4 Preheat a 7-litre air fryer to 160°C/325°F for 3 minutes.

5 Taking care, place the dish in the air fryer basket; at 160°C/325°F, cook for 25 minutes until potatoes are just tender.
6 Scatter potatoes with gruyère; at 160°C/325°F, cook for a further 5 minutes or until cheese is golden.
7 Sprinkle potato gratin with salt flakes to serve.

prep + cook time 45 minutes
serves 6

LOADED CORN

6 corn cobs (1.5kg), in husks
100g (3oz) fresh goat's cheese,
    crumbled
finely grated rind of 1 lime
¼ cup coriander (cilantro) leaves
¼ cup (20g) asian fried shallots
to serve: lime wedges

SRIRACHA & LIME BUTTER
125g (4oz) butter, chopped, softened
¼ cup (70g) sriracha chilli sauce
2 tsp lime juice

1 Cook corn in their husks in a large saucepan of boiling salted water for 3 minutes or until almost tender; drain. Cool. Peel back husks; remove and discard silks. Tie the husks back with kitchen string.
2 Preheat a 5.3-litre air fryer to 200°C/400°F for 3 minutes.
3 Bend husks back so corn will fit in the air fryer basket; wrap just the husks in foil to prevent burning.
4 Taking care, place half the corn cobs in the air fryer basket; at 200°C/400°F, cook for 10 minutes. Transfer to a plate; cover to keep warm. Repeat cooking with remaining corn cobs.

5 Meanwhile, to make sriracha and lime butter, process butter in a small food processor until whipped. Add sriracha and lime juice; process until smooth.
6 Spread sriracha and lime butter on hot corn; top with goat's cheese, lime rind, coriander and fried shallots. Serve with lime wedges.

prep + cook time 35 minutes
makes 6

ASPARAGUS
WITH PROSCIUTTO
& GARLIC BUTTER

24 asparagus spears (600g), trimmed
4 slices prosciutto (60g),
  halved lengthways
olive oil cooking spray
30g (1oz) butter
1 clove garlic, crushed
2 tsp thyme leaves

1 Preheat a 7-litre air fryer to 180°C/350°F for 3 minutes.
2 Group asparagus into bundles of three spears each. Wrap a slice of prosciutto around each bundle to secure; spray all over with oil.
3 Taking care, place asparagus bundles in the air fryer basket; at 180°C/350°F, cook for 6 minutes, turning halfway through cooking time, until prosciutto is golden and asparagus are tender.

4 Meanwhile, to make garlic butter, cook butter and garlic in a small frying pan over medium heat until butter is melted; stir in thyme. Season with salt and freshly ground pepper.
5 Serve asparagus bundles drizzled with garlic butter.

prep + cook time 15 minutes
serves 4

HASSELBACK SWEET POTATOES

6 mini orange sweet potatoes (1.2kg)
60g (2oz) butter, melted
2 cloves garlic, crushed
½ tsp ground cinnamon
2 tsp salt flakes
100g (3oz) round mild sliced pancetta
1 tbsp chopped chives

WHIPPED CHIVE BUTTER
80g (2½oz) butter, softened
1 tsp maple syrup
2 tbsp chopped chives

1 Wash unpeeled sweet potatoes; place on a chopping board. Trim a little piece lengthways from one side so they sit flat. Place a chopstick on the board along each side of a sweet potato. Slice crossways at 1cm (½in) intervals, cutting through to the chopsticks (the chopsticks will prevent you from cutting all the way through). Repeat with remaining sweet potatoes.
2 Preheat a 5.3-litre air fryer to 200°C/400°F for 3 minutes.
3 Combine butter, garlic, cinnamon and salt flakes in a small bowl. Brush butter mixture over sweet potatoes.
4 Taking care, place sweet potatoes in the air fryer basket; at 200°C/400°F, cook for 15 minutes.

5 Place pancetta on top of sweet potatoes; at 200°C/400°F, cook for a further 5 minutes until sweet potatoes are tender when pierced with the tip of a knife and the pancetta is crisp.
6 Meanwhile, to make whipped chive butter, beat butter in a small bowl with an electric mixer until light and fluffy. Beat in maple syrup, then stir in chives.
7 Spread sweet potatoes with whipped chive butter. Serve topped with crisp pancetta and chopped chives.

swap it You can use any type of sweet potato or even regular potatoes. If using regular potatoes, omit the cinnamon and use paprika instead. Regular potatoes will discolour when cut, so prepare close to serving.

prep + cook time 1 hour
serves 6

PREP IT Sweet potatoes can be prepared to the end of step 3 up to 6 hours ahead; refrigerate until required. Preheat the air fryer just before cooking.

spicy cajun potato wedges

paprika potato wedges

sweet potato wedges

lemon pepper fries

chilli garlic fries

salted fries

SPICY CAJUN POTATO WEDGES

Preheat a 5.3-litre air fryer to 200°C/400°F for 3 minutes. Cut 1kg (2lb) unpeeled kipfler (fingerling) potatoes into wedges. Combine 2 tbsp olive oil, ½ tsp ground oregano, 2 tsp ground cumin, 1 tsp hot paprika, ½ tsp ground black pepper, 1 tsp ground coriander and ¼ tsp chilli powder in a large bowl. Add wedges and toss to coat. Place wedges in the air fryer basket; cook for 15–20 minutes, turning once, or until golden and cooked. Season with salt and serve topped with oregano leaves.

PAPRIKA POTATO WEDGES

Preheat a 5.3-litre air fryer to 200°C/400°F for 3 minutes. Cut 1kg (2lb) floury potatoes (sebago) into wedges. Place in a large bowl with 2 tbsp extra virgin olive oil, 40g (1½oz) melted butter and 2 tsp smoked paprika. Season with salt and toss to coat. Place wedges in the air fryer basket; cook for 15–20 minutes, turning once, or until golden and cooked. Scatter with ½ cup (40g) finely grated parmesan and serve with garlic mayonnaise.

6 WAYS HAND-CUT CHIPS & WEDGES

SWEET POTATO WEDGES WITH CHILLI LIME SALT

Preheat a 5.3-litre air fryer to 200°C/400°F for 3 minutes. Cut 1kg (2lb) orange sweet potatoes into wedges. Toss with 2 tbsp olive oil. Place wedges in the air fryer basket; cook for 15–20 minutes, turning once, or until golden and cooked. Combine 2 tsp finely grated lime rind, 2 tbsp salt flakes and 1 tsp chilli flakes in a small heatproof bowl; place in air fryer for the last 3 minutes of cooking time to dry out the rind. Sprinkle wedges with chilli lime salt to serve.

SALTED FRIES

Cut 1kg (2lb) peeled russet burbank potatoes lengthways into 1cm (½in) thick slices, then cut slices lengthways into 1cm (½in) thick batons. Place in a large bowl of cold water. Stand for 30 minutes; drain, then pat dry with paper towel. Toss with 2 tbsp olive oil. Preheat a 5.3-litre air fryer to 200°C/400°F for 3 minutes. Place fries in the air fryer basket; cook for 15–20 minutes, turning once, or until golden and cooked. Season with salt.

LEMON PEPPER FRIES

Make a batch of Salted Fries (below left), omitting the salt. Combine 1 tbsp finely grated lemon rind, ½ tsp freshly ground black pepper and 1 tsp salt flakes in a small bowl. Sprinkle hot fries with lemon pepper and serve with lemon wedges.

swap it Use grated lime rind instead of lemon rind and crushed sichuan peppercorns instead of black pepper.

serving suggestion These fries go well with battered or grilled fish, or with fish sandwiches, prawns and chicken.

CHILLI GARLIC FRIES

Make a batch of Salted Fries (left). Heat 2 tsp olive oil in a small frying pan. Cook 2 sliced long red chillies until soft. Add 2 sliced cloves garlic; cook, stirring, until fragrant. Sprinkle hot fries with chilli mixture to serve.

serving suggestion These fries go well with hamburgers, grilled or pan-fried steak and lamb cutlets.

BEETROOT
WITH YOGHURT
& DUKKAH

700g (1½lb) mixed baby beetroot
(beets), scrubbed, unpeeled (see tip)
2 tbsp extra virgin olive oil
1½ tbsp dukkah spice mix
½ cup (140g) greek yoghurt
1 tbsp lemon juice
to serve: extra virgin olive oil and
flat-leaf parsley leaves

1 Preheat a 7-litre air fryer to 180°C/350°F for 3 minutes.

2 Quarter, halve or cut beetroot into wedges so that all the pieces are a similar size. Place beetroot and oil in a large bowl; season. Using your fingers, massage the oil into each beetroot wedge (wear gloves if you don't want to stain your hands).

3 Taking care, place beetroot, cut-side up, in the air fryer basket; at 180°C/350°F, cook for 25 minutes, turning a number of times, until tender. Scatter dukkah over beetroot for the last 5 minutes of cooking time.

4 Meanwhile, combine yoghurt and lemon juice in a small bowl; season to taste.

5 To serve, spread yoghurt mixture on a plate or platter; top with dukkah-spiced beetroot. Drizzle with extra olive oil and scatter with flat-leaf parsley leaves. Sprinkle with any dukkah that may have fallen through the basket holes into the pan.

prep + cook time 35 minutes
serves 4

TIP You can also use regular size beetroot, cut into 1.5cm (¾in) wedges.

EPIC JACKET POTATOES

8 coliban potatoes (2.4kg) or 4 small
  orange sweet potatoes (1kg)
extra virgin olive oil cooking spray
½ tsp salt flakes
to serve: butter

1 Preheat a 5.3-litre air fryer to 200°C/400°F for 3 minutes.

2 Prick potatoes all over with a fork. Taking care, place potatoes in the air fryer basket, then spray with oil and sprinkle with salt flakes; at 200°C/400°F, cook for 40 minutes, turning halfway through cooking time, until tender when pierced with the tip of a knife.

3 Transfer potatoes to plates. Cut a cross in the top of each potato, then squeeze upwards from the bottom to open up. Serve with lashings of butter or with one of the toppers.

TOPPERS

nachos Heat a 425g (13½oz) can mexe beans in a small saucepan. Top jacket potatoes with 25g (¾oz) corn chips, then the beans; scatter with 1 cup (120g) grated cheddar. Return topped potatoes to the air fryer basket; at 200°C/400°F, cook for 2 minutes until cheese melts. To serve, top potatoes with ½ cup (120g) sour cream, 1 fresh sliced jalapeño chilli and ¼ cup coriander (cilantro) leaves. Drizzle with your favourite chilli sauce. Season to taste.

baked barbecue beans Place 250g (8oz) halved cherry tomatoes in a medium saucepan with a 420g (13½oz) can baked beans, 1 tablespoon dijon mustard and 1 tablespoon smoky barbecue sauce; cook over medium heat, stirring occasionally, until mixture is heated through. To serve, top jacket potatoes with baked bean mixture and ¼ cup (20g) finely grated parmesan. Season to taste.

tip To reduce the air fryer time, par-cook the potatoes first. Prick them all over with a fork, then microwave on HIGH (100%) for 8 minutes or until soft. Bake in the air fryer for 15 minutes.

prep + cook time 45 minutes
serves 4

SESAME & CHILLI-BAKED BROCCOLINI WITH MUSHROOMS

2 bunches broccolini (700g), trimmed
2 long red chillies, seeded, sliced thickly
200g (6½oz) mixed mushrooms,
    sliced (see tip)
1 tbsp sesame oil
3 cloves garlic, sliced thinly
1 tbsp sesame seeds
2 tbsp oyster sauce

1 Preheat a 7-litre air fryer to 180°C/350°F for 3 minutes.

2 Combine broccolini, chilli and mushrooms in a large bowl, then add sesame oil; toss to coat. Season.

3 Taking care, place vegetable mixture in the air fryer basket; at 180°C/350°F, cook for 10 minutes, tossing halfway through cooking time, or until vegetables are beginning to crisp at edges.

4 Sprinkle vegetables with garlic and sesame seeds; at 180°C/350°F, cook for a further 3 minutes until tender.

5 Serve vegetables drizzled with oyster sauce.

tip We used shiitake, king, oyster and button mushrooms.

prep + cook time 25 minutes
serves 4

PARMESAN, THYME & CARROT RÖSTI

2 medium carrots (240g),
   grated coarsely
1 medium starchy potato (200g),
   grated coarsely
½ small onion (40g), grated coarsely
2 eggs, beaten lightly
⅓ cup (25g) finely grated parmesan
1 tbsp cornflour (cornstarch)
1 tbsp finely chopped thyme leaves
1 clove garlic, crushed
olive oil cooking spray
to serve: sea salt flakes and sour cream

1 Preheat a 7-litre air fryer to 200°C/400°F for 3 minutes.

2 Combine carrot, potato, onion, egg, parmesan, cornflour, thyme and garlic in a large bowl, then season; mix well. Shape carrot mixture into eight 1cm (½in) thick round rösti, pressing each firmly between hands to compact; spray all over with oil.

3 Spray the air fryer basket with oil. Taking care, place rösti in the basket; at 180°C/350°F, cook for 14 minutes, turning halfway through cooking time, until golden and tender.

4 Sprinkle rösti with salt flakes and serve with sour cream.

prep + cook time 35 minutes
serves 4 (makes 8)

163

PUMPKIN WITH
SAGE &
FETTA

800g (1½lb) kent pumpkin, unpeeled,
    cut into 1.5cm (¾in) wedges
2 tbsp extra virgin olive oil
1 bunch sage, leaves picked
60g (2oz) fetta, crumbled
⅓ cup (35g) walnut halves, roasted,
    chopped coarsely
to serve: balsamic vinegar and
    extra virgin olive oil

1 Preheat a 7-litre
air fryer to 200°C/400°F
for 3 minutes.
2 Place pumpkin and oil in
a large bowl; season. Using
your fingers, massage the oil
into each pumpkin wedge.
Reserve remaining oil in bowl.
3 Taking care, place pumpkin
upright in the air fryer basket;
at 200°C/400°F, cook for
25 minutes, turning a number
of times, until tender.
4 Meanwhile, place sage
leaves in reserved bowl and
rub with remaining oil. Place
sage in and around pumpkin
pieces for the last 5 minutes
of cooking time.

5 Top pumpkin with sage,
fetta and walnuts. Serve
drizzled with balsamic vinegar
and a little extra olive oil.

prep + cook time 40 minutes
serves 4

POLENTA ZUCCHINI CHIPS WITH AÏOLI

1 egg
½ cup (85g) polenta
⅓ cup (25g) finely grated parmesan
1 tsp garlic salt
2 large zucchini (300g), cut into
    1cm (½in) thick batons
olive oil cooking spray
½ cup (150g) whole-egg mayonnaise
1 tbsp lemon juice
2 cloves garlic, crushed
¼ cup finely chopped chives
to serve: sea salt flakes

1 Lightly beat egg in a large bowl. Combine polenta, parmesan and garlic salt in another large bowl, then season with pepper. Add zucchini batons to egg and toss to coat, then dust in polenta mixture, shaking off excess; spray all over with oil.
2 Preheat a 7-litre air fryer to 200°C/400°F for 3 minutes.
3 Spray the air fryer basket generously with oil. Taking care, place half the zucchini chips in the basket; at 200°C/400°F, cook for 12 minutes, turning halfway through cooking time, until golden and tender. Transfer to a plate; cover loosely with foil to keep warm. Repeat cooking with remaining zucchini chips.

4 Meanwhile, to make aïoli, combine mayonnaise, lemon juice, garlic and 2 tablespoons of the chives in a small bowl; season.
5 Sprinkle zucchini chips with salt flakes and remaining chives. Serve with aïoli.

prep + cook time 30 minutes
serves 4

CRISP TOFU
WITH PALM
SUGAR DRESSING

600g (1lb) medium tofu

2 bunches broccolini (700g), trimmed,
   thick stems halved lengthways

170g (5½oz) gai lan, trimmed,
   cut into 5cm (2in) lengths

3 egg whites

1 cup (180g) rice flour

2 tbsp sesame seeds

1 tbsp ground white pepper

2 tsp freshly ground black pepper

2 tsp salt

olive oil cooking spray

to serve: sliced green onions (scallions),
   sliced red chilli, extra sesame seeds
   and lime cheeks

PALM SUGAR DRESSING

1 tbsp finely grated ginger

¼ cup (60ml) extra virgin olive oil

2 tbsp lime juice

¼ cup (60ml) mirin

¼ cup (60ml) soy sauce

1 tbsp finely grated palm sugar

1 small red chilli, chopped finely

1 Cut tofu horizontally into four slices; cut each slice in half to make eight pieces in total. Line a board with paper towel. Place tofu slices on paper towel; lay more paper towel on top of tofu, then top with a heavy tray (or small chopping board) to weigh the tofu down. Leave for 10 minutes to drain.

2 Preheat a 5.3-litre air fryer to 180°C/350°F for 3 minutes.

3 Rinse broccolini and gai lan. Taking care, place damp vegetables in the air fryer basket; at 180°C/350°F, cook for 5 minutes until just tender. Transfer to a platter; cover to keep warm.

4 Meanwhile, to make palm sugar dressing, place ingredients in a screw-top jar; shake well to combine.

5 Beat egg whites in a shallow bowl. Combine rice flour, sesame seeds, peppers and salt in a second shallow bowl. Dip tofu slices in egg white, then coat in rice flour mixture; spray generously with oil.

6 Place half the tofu in the basket; at 180°C/350°F, cook for 15 minutes, turning halfway through cooking time, or until crisp and golden. Transfer to a wire rack. Repeat cooking with remaining tofu.

7 Top vegetables with crisp tofu, sliced green onion, sliced chilli and extra sesame seeds; drizzle with dressing. Serve with lime cheeks.

prep + cook time 45 minutes
serves 4

WEEKENDS

The air fryer might be the
best appliance for fast and
easy cooking during the week,
but it's also a superstar when
it comes to cooking larger
cuts of meat and fish as well
as more ambitious recipes.

STEAK
WITH BÉARNAISE
& FRIES

600g (1¼lb) red-skinned potatoes,
   cut into 1cm (½in) chips
olive oil cooking spray
4 x 200g (6½oz) beef scotch fillet
   steaks (2cm/¾in thick)
2 cups (240g) frozen peas

BÉARNAISE SAUCE
½ cup (125ml) dry white wine
2 tbsp white wine vinegar
2 shallots (50g), chopped finely
1 tsp dried tarragon
1 tsp black peppercorns
3 egg yolks
250g (8oz) butter, melted
1 tbsp finely chopped fresh tarragon

1 To make béarnaise sauce, combine wine, vinegar, shallots, dried tarragon and peppercorns in a small saucepan; simmer for 5 minutes or until liquid reduces to about 2 tablespoons. Strain through a fine sieve into a heatproof bowl; discard the shallot mixture. Place bowl containing wine mixture over a saucepan of simmering water (make sure the bowl doesn't touch the water). Add egg yolks to the bowl; whisk for 3 minutes or until mixture is pale and frothy. Add butter 1 tablespoon at a time, whisking continuously after each addition until sauce is thick and smooth. Remove from heat. Stir in fresh tarragon; season. Cover pan and set aside.

2 Preheat an 11-litre air fryer to 200°C/400°F for 3 minutes.

3 Spray potato chips all over with oil and spread out on two of the air fryer racks.

4 Taking care, slide the racks onto the lower shelves of the air fryer; at 200°C/400°F, cook for 20 minutes, rotating racks halfway through cooking time.

5 Place steaks on the remaining rack. Spray both sides with oil and season. Taking care, slide the rack into the second highest shelf of the air fryer; at 200°C/400°F, cook for 7 minutes, turning after 2 minutes, or until steaks are medium or cooked to your liking and potato chips are golden and tender. Transfer steaks to a plate; cover loosely with foil and rest for 5 minutes.

6 Meanwhile, boil, steam or microwave peas until just tender; drain.

7 Season steaks with freshly ground black pepper. Serve with béarnaise sauce, chips and peas.

prep + cook time 1 hour
serves 4

TIPS Do not position the steaks on the highest shelf in the air fryer, as this can cause the appliance to smoke. For a smaller 7-litre air fryer, cook the potato chips first, then transfer to a plate while you cook the steaks. While the steaks are resting, reheat the chips in the air fryer.

BLUEBERRY PIE BAKED PORRIDGE

½ cup (45g) traditional rolled oats
½ tsp ground ginger
pinch salt flakes
1 tbsp brown sugar
2 tbsp dry-roasted almonds,
   chopped coarsely
1 cup (250ml) milk
1 tbsp honey
1 tsp extra virgin olive oil
125g (4oz) blueberries, halved or whole
2 corella pears (200g), halved,
   cored, cut into wedges
1 cup (280g) greek yoghurt
to serve: ground cinnamon

1 Preheat a 5.3-litre air fryer to 160°C/325°F for 3 minutes. Grease a 1-litre (4-cup) ovenproof dish; ensure the dish will fit into the air fryer.
2 Combine oats, ginger, salt flakes, sugar and half the almonds in the dish. Whisk milk, half the honey and the oil in a large jug until combined; add to oat mixture, stirring until just combined. Fold in half the blueberries and two-thirds of the pears. Spread mixture evenly in the dish; cover tightly with foil.
3 Taking care, place dish in the air fryer basket; at 160°C/325°F, cook for 20 minutes until oats are tender. Stand dish in the air fryer for 5 minutes.

4 Serve porridge topped with yoghurt and remaining blueberries, pears and almonds, drizzled with remaining honey and dusted with cinnamon.

prep + cook time 35 minutes
serves 2

MAPLE BACON WRAPPED MINI MEATLOAVES

½ small onion (40g), grated finely
⅓ cup finely chopped flat-leaf parsley
2 cloves garlic, crushed
½ cup (50g) packaged breadcrumbs
1 egg, beaten lightly
¼ cup (70g) low-sugar tomato sauce (ketchup)
1 tbsp worcestershire sauce
500g (1lb) minced (ground) beef
1 tbsp chopped thyme leaves
4 rindless bacon rashers (250g)
½ tbsp maple syrup
to serve: extra low-sugar tomato sauce (ketchup)

1 Preheat a 7-litre air fryer to 180°C/350°F for 3 minutes.

2 Combine onion, parsley, garlic, breadcrumbs, egg, sauces and beef in a large bowl, then season; mix well to combine. Divide mixture into four even portions and shape each into a small loaf. Sprinkle with thyme, then wrap in bacon.

3 Taking care, place meatloaves, top-side down, in the air fryer basket; at 180°C/350°F, cook for 20 minutes, turning halfway through cooking time. Brush tops with maple syrup during the last 5 minutes of cooking time.

4 Serve meatloaves with extra tomato sauce.

serve it Wrap meatloaves in cos or iceberg lettuce leaves for a crunchy finish.

prep + cook time 40 minutes
serves 4

MATCH IT Peri Peri Potatoes, page 195.

SPICY KOREAN PEANUT PORK RIBS

2kg (4lb) American-style pork ribs
2 cloves garlic, crushed
1 tsp finely grated ginger
¼ cup (95g) crunchy peanut butter
1 tbsp sriracha chilli sauce
1 tbsp soy sauce
2 tsp fish sauce
1 tbsp brown sugar
2 tsp sesame oil
2 tbsp lime juice
½ cup (125ml) coconut cream
cooking oil spray
2 lebanese cucumbers, seeded,
    halved lengthways, sliced thinly
2 long red chillies, chopped finely
to serve: lime wedges and
    steamed jasmine rice

1 Using a small, sharp knife, remove the layer of membrane from the back of the ribs (or ask the butcher to do this for you). Place ribs in a large saucepan and cover well with water; bring to the boil over medium heat. Reduce heat; simmer for 45 minutes or until almost tender.

2 Meanwhile, to make marinade, place garlic, ginger, peanut butter, sauces, sugar, oil and half the lime juice in a blender or small food processor; blend until smooth. Add coconut cream; blend until combined. Transfer to a large non-metallic dish. Drain ribs; add to marinade and turn to coat. Cover dish. Refrigerate for 2 hours.

3 Preheat a 7-litre air fryer to 180°C/350°F for 3 minutes.

4 Spray the air fryer basket with oil. Remove ribs from the marinade, scraping off any that has solidified; reserve remaining marinade. Taking care, arrange the ribs in the basket, standing them up and leaning them against the side of the basket and one another. Reset the temperature to 160°C/325°F; cook for 20 minutes.

5 Brush ribs with a third of the reserved marinade; at 160°C/325°F, cook for a further 10 minutes until tender and glazed.

6 Meanwhile, combine cucumber, chilli and remaining lime juice in a small bowl; season. Stand for 10 minutes.

7 To make peanut sauce, place remaining reserved marinade and 2 tablespoons water in a small saucepan over medium-high heat; bring to the boil. Reduce heat; simmer for 4 minutes or until thickened slightly.

8 Cut ribs into serving-sized pieces and place on a large platter; spoon over a little peanut sauce. Serve with remaining peanut sauce, the cucumber mixture, lime wedges and rice.

prep + cook time
1 hour 40 minutes
(+ refrigeration)
serves 4

CHICKEN & LEEK PIE

2 cups (500ml) chicken stock
625g (1¼lb) chicken breast fillets
2 sheets frozen butter puff pastry,
    just thawed
1 egg, beaten lightly
cooking oil spray
60g (2oz) butter
1 large leek (500g), sliced thinly
2 stalks celery (300g), trimmed,
    chopped finely
2 tbsp plain (all-purpose) flour
2 tsp thyme leaves
½ cup (125ml) milk
1 cup (250ml) pouring cream
2 tsp wholegrain mustard

1 Bring stock to the boil in a medium saucepan. Add chicken; return to the boil. Reduce heat; simmer, covered, for 10 minutes or until chicken is cooked through. Remove from heat. Stand chicken in poaching liquid for 10 minutes.

2 Preheat a 5.3-litre air fryer to 180°C/350°F for 3 minutes.

3 Stack pastry sheets on top of one another. Place a 15cm x 22cm (6in x 8¾in), 1.5-litre (6-cup) rectangular dish over pastry stack; cut around it to cut out a rectangle the same size, then cut four slits crossways in the centre of the pastry. (Alternatively, use another sized dish but no larger than the pastry sheet.)

4 Brush pastry with egg. Spray the air fryer basket with oil. Taking care, place pastry stack in the basket; at 180°C/350°F, cook for 15–18 minutes until pastry is puffed and deep golden.

5 Meanwhile, remove chicken from liquid; chop coarsely. Reserve 1 cup (250ml) of the poaching liquid. (Keep remaining liquid for another use or discard.) Heat butter in a medium saucepan; cook leek and celery, stirring, until leek softens. Add flour and thyme; cook, stirring, for 1 minute. Gradually stir in reserved poaching liquid, the milk and cream; cook, stirring, until mixture boils and thickens. Stir in chopped chicken and the mustard. Season to taste.

6 Spoon hot chicken mixture into dish; carefully place cooked puff pastry on top. Serve pie scattered with extra thyme, if you like.

prep + cook time 45 minutes
serves 6

PREP IT Pie filling can be made a day ahead; refrigerate until required.

TIP If you can't find sun-dried tomatoes without oil, use marinated ones or semi-dried tomatoes.

STUFFED CAPSICUMS

¾ cup (180ml) vegetable stock, boiling
2 tbsp extra virgin olive oil
1 cup (200g) wholemeal couscous
1 large red onion (300g), chopped finely
2 tsp dried oregano
250g (8oz) cherry tomatoes, halved
4 large mixed capsicums (bell peppers)
    (1.4kg)
125g (4oz) sun-dried tomatoes,
    no-added oil, halved (see tip)
⅓ cup (60g) kalamata olives, halved
1 tsp finely grated lemon rind
2 tbsp lemon juice
⅓ cup (65g) pepitas (pumpkin seed
    kernels), toasted
½ cup oregano leaves (optional)

BASIL & ROCKET YOGHURT
2 cups basil leaves
1 cup baby rocket (arugula) leaves
¾ cup (210g) greek yoghurt

1 Preheat a 5.3-litre air fryer to 180°C/350°F for 3 minutes.

2 Place boiling stock and 1 tablespoon of the oil in a heatproof bowl; stir in couscous. Cover and stand for 5 minutes or until liquid is absorbed. Fluff couscous with a fork.

3 Meanwhile, taking care, line the air fryer basket with foil. Layer on top of the foil the onion, dried oregano and cherry tomatoes, then drizzle with remaining oil; at 180°C/350°F, cook for 5 minutes until tomatoes are softened.

4 Meanwhile, cut the top off each capsicum and remove the seeds and membrane; reserve the tops. Combine couscous, tomato mixture, sun-dried tomatoes and olives in a bowl. Add lemon rind and lemon juice; mix to combine. Season to taste. Fill capsicum bases with couscous mixture.

5 Wrap stuffed capsicum bases individually in foil and place in the basket; at 180°C/350°F, cook for 20 minutes. Remove capsicum bases from the basket and unwrap; place capsicum tops on bases, then wrap again in foil. Return stuffed capsicums to the basket; cook for a further 20 minutes until capsicums are cooked through.

6 Meanwhile, to make basil and rocket yoghurt, place basil and rocket in a heatproof bowl; cover with boiling water. Stand for 1 minute; drain. Cool under cold running water. Squeeze out excess liquid. Blend with yoghurt until smooth. Season to taste.

7 Serve stuffed capsicums topped with basil and rocket yoghurt, toasted pepitas and oregano.

prep + cook time 1¼ hours
makes 4

BUTTERFLIED HARISSA CHICKEN WITH COUSCOUS & ORANGE

1.4kg (2¾lb) whole chicken
2 cloves garlic, crushed
2 tbsp lemon juice
2 tsp sweet paprika
1 tbsp harissa paste (see tip)
2 tbsp extra virgin olive oil
olive oil cooking spray
1 cup (200g) couscous
1 cup (250ml) boiling water
½ cup coriander (cilantro) leaves
2 medium oranges (480g),
    peeled, sliced thinly
to serve: greek yoghurt and
    sea salt flakes

1 Place chicken, breast-side down, on a board. Using poultry shears, cut down both sides of the backbone and discard. Open out the chicken, turn it over and press down on the breastbone with the heel of your hand to flatten.

2 Combine garlic, lemon juice, paprika, harissa and oil in a large shallow dish; add chicken and turn to coat. Cover dish. Refrigerate for at least 2 hours or overnight.

3 Preheat a 7-litre air fryer to 180°C/350°F for 5 minutes.

4 Spray the air fryer basket with oil. Taking care, place chicken, skin-side up, in the basket, then cover loosely with foil; at 180°C/350°F, cook for 20 minutes.

5 Remove foil; cook chicken for a further 20 minutes until juices run clear when a skewer is inserted into the thickest part of a thigh. Transfer to a dish; cover with foil and rest for 10 minutes.

6 Meanwhile, combine couscous and the boiling water in a large heatproof bowl; cover and stand for 5 minutes or until liquid is absorbed. Fluff couscous with a fork. Stir in coriander and season to taste.

7 Serve chicken with couscous, oranges and yoghurt; drizzle with any cooking juices from the bottom of the air fryer pan. Sprinkle with salt flakes.

tip Harissa brands can vary in heat, so use according to taste.

prep + cook time 1 hour (+ refrigeration & standing)
serves 4

GARLIC PRAWNS & SCALLOPS

800g (1½lb) uncooked prawns (shrimp),
    peeled, deveined, tails intact
4 cloves garlic, sliced thinly
¼ cup (60ml) extra virgin olive oil
½ cup flat-leaf parsley
1 long red chilli, sliced thinly
8 scallops on the half-shell
finely grated rind of 1 lime
to serve: thinly sliced toasted bread
    (see tip), lemon wedges and
    Chilli & Lime Mayo (see page 101)
    or bought aïoli

1 Preheat a 5.3-litre air fryer to 180C°/350°F for 3 minutes.

2 Place prawns on a piece of baking paper slightly larger than the base of the air fryer basket.

3 Combine garlic, oil, parsley and chilli in a small bowl. Spoon two-thirds of the garlic oil mixture over the prawns; toss to combine. Reserve remaining garlic oil mixture in bowl.

4 Taking care, lower the prawns, on the paper, into the air fryer basket; at 180°C/350°F, cook for 6 minutes.

5 Turn prawns over, placing the more cooked ones towards the centre of the basket; cook for a further 6 minutes until cooked through. Lift prawns, on the paper, out of the basket. Transfer prawns and any cooking juices to a platter; cover to keep warm.

6 Drizzle scallops with reserved garlic oil mixture. Place scallops, on their shells, in the basket (there is no need to line the basket); at 180°C/350°F, cook for 3 minutes until scallops just turn opaque.

7 Add scallops to the platter and scatter with lime rind. Serve prawns and scallops with toast, lemon wedges and Chilli & Lime Mayo.

tip The air fryer makes great crunchy toast or croûtons from leftover bread. Thinly slice bread with a serrated knife. Spray both sides with olive oil cooking spray. Place in a preheated 180°C/350°F air fryer for 5 minutes or until golden and crisp.

prep + cook time 30 minutes
serves 4

ROAST PORK BELLY

WITH FENNEL & CHILLI SALT

2 tsp fennel seeds
2 tsp sea salt flakes
2 tsp dried chilli flakes
2 tsp finely grated lemon rind
2 cloves garlic, crushed
1 tbsp olive oil
1kg (2lb) piece boneless pork belly, rind scored
to serve: extra sea salt flakes, roast potatoes and roast shallots

1 Preheat a 7-litre air fryer to 180°C/350°F for 3 minutes.

2 Place fennel seeds, salt and chilli flakes in a mortar and pestle; crush lightly. Add lemon rind, garlic and oil; pound to combine. Pat pork belly rind dry with paper towel. Rub fennel mixture all over pork.

3 Taking care, place pork, skin-side up, in the air fryer basket. Reset temperature to 200°C/400°F; cook for 25 minutes until skin crackles.

4 Reset the temperature to 160°C/325°F; cook pork for a further 25 minutes until tender, or until an internal temperature of 70°C–75°C/160°F–170°F is reached on a meat thermometer. (If pork is overbrowning, cover with foil.)

5 Thickly slice pork and season with extra salt flakes. Serve with any cooking juices from the bottom of the air fryer pan, roast potatoes and roast shallots.

prep + cook time 1 hour
serves 4

MATCH IT Roast Potatoes 4 Ways, page 195, or Italian-style Rice Salad, page 132.

testing meat

Insert a meat thermometer into the thickest part of the beef. The internal temperature should reach:

rare 55–60°C/130–140°F
medium–rare
60–65°C/140–150°F
medium
65–70°C/150–160°F
medium–well done
70–75°C/160–170°F
well done 75°C/170°F

HERB-CRUSTED ROAST BEEF WITH CREAMY MUSHROOMS

1.2kg (2½lb) piece beef scotch fillet
1 tbsp olive oil
⅔ cup (80g) panko (japanese) breadcrumbs
¼ cup (20g) finely grated parmesan
2 tbsp chopped flat-leaf parsley
1 tbsp chopped tarragon
¼ cup chopped chives
3 cloves garlic, crushed
¼ cup (70g) wholegrain mustard
1 tsp smoked paprika
olive oil cooking spray
150g (4½oz) swiss brown mushrooms, halved (or quartered if large)
150g (4½oz) button mushrooms, halved (or quartered if large)
¾ cup (180ml) thickened (heavy) cream
to serve: roast potatoes

1 Preheat a 7-litre air fryer to 200°C/400°F for 5 minutes.
2 Brush beef with 2 teaspoons of the oil and season.
3 Taking care, place beef in the air fryer basket; at 200°C/400°F, cook for 15 minutes, turning halfway through cooking time, until browned all over.
4 Meanwhile, combine the breadcrumbs, parmesan, parsley, tarragon, half the chives and half the garlic in a bowl; season. Transfer beef to a plate and pat dry with paper towel. Working quickly, spread 2 tablespoons of the mustard over the top and sides of beef, sprinkle with paprika, then firmly press on breadcrumb mixture. Spray breadcrumbs generously with oil.
5 Return beef to the air fryer basket. Cover basket tightly with foil. Reset the temperature to 180°C/350°F; cook for 30 minutes. Remove foil.

6 Toss mushrooms in remaining oil and add to the air fryer basket; at 180°C/350°F, cook, without foil, for a further 10 minutes until beef is medium or cooked to your liking (see Testing Meat to left) and mushrooms are browned. Transfer beef to a dish; cover loosely with foil and rest for 15 minutes.
7 Meanwhile, to make creamy mushrooms, combine cream and remaining garlic and mustard in a medium saucepan over medium heat. Add the mushrooms and any cooking juices from the bottom of the air fryer pan; bring to the boil. Reduce heat; simmer, stirring occasionally, for 5 minutes or until sauce thickens slightly. Stir in remaining chives and season to taste.
8 Thinly slice beef and serve with creamy mushrooms and roast potatoes.

match it Roast Potatoes 4 Ways, page 195.

prep + cook time 1 hour 20 minutes
serves 6

TIKKA LAMB CUTLETS WITH CARROT KOSHIMBIR

⅓ cup (80g) bottled tikka paste
1 tbsp lemon juice
½ cup (140g) greek yoghurt
12 french-trimmed lamb cutlets (600g)
olive oil cooking spray
to serve: steamed basmati rice
    and warm naan bread

CARROT KOSHIMBIR
2 medium carrots (240g),
    grated coarsely
⅓ cup (25g) shredded coconut
¼ cup firmly packed coriander
    (cilantro) leaves
1 long green chilli, sliced thinly
2 tbsp lemon juice

1 Combine tikka paste, lemon juice and half the yoghurt in a large bowl; add lamb and toss to coat. Refrigerate for 1 hour.
2 Preheat a 7-litre air fryer to 200°C/400°F for 3 minutes.
3 To make carrot koshimbir, place carrot, coconut, half the coriander, the chilli and lemon juice in a bowl; mix well. Season.
4 Taking care, line the air fryer basket with a silicone mat, if available (see page 11). Spray lamb generously on both sides with oil and place in the basket; at 200°C/400°F, cook for 8 minutes, turning halfway through cooking time, for medium or until cooked to your liking.

5 Meanwhile, finely chop remaining coriander (from carrot koshimbir) and stir into remaining yoghurt.
6 Serve lamb cutlets with steamed rice, warm naan bread, carrot koshimbir and coriander yoghurt.

prep + cook time 20 minutes (+ refrigeration)
serves 4

Greek-style potatoes

mustard & mint potatoes

4 WAYS

peri peri potatoes

fetta, dill & bacon potatoes

ROAST POTATOES

GREEK-STYLE POTATOES

Preheat a 7-litre air fryer to 200°C/400°F for 3 minutes. Cut 1kg (2lb) baby red-skinned potatoes into quarters lengthways. Place in a large bowl with 2 tbsp olive oil, 2 tsp dried oregano, 2 tbsp finely chopped rosemary and 4 crushed cloves garlic, then season; mix well to coat. Taking care, place potatoes in the air fryer basket; at 200°C/400°F, cook for 20 minutes, turning halfway through cooking time, until golden and tender. Serve drizzled with 2 tbsp lemon juice.

MUSTARD & MINT POTATOES

Preheat a 7-litre air fryer to 200°C/400°F for 3 minutes. Cut 1kg (2lb) baby red-skinned potatoes in half lengthways. Place in a large bowl with 2 tbsp olive oil, then season; mix well to coat. Taking care, place potatoes in the air fryer basket; at 200°C/400°F, cook for 20 minutes, turning halfway through cooking time, until golden and tender. Meanwhile, combine 1 tsp each dijon mustard and wholegrain mustard, 2 tbsp finely chopped mint, 1 tbsp olive oil and 3 tsp white wine vinegar in a large bowl; add potatoes and toss to coat. Serve scattered with mint leaves.

PERI PERI POTATOES

Preheat a 7-litre air fryer to 200°C/400°F for 3 minutes. Cut 1kg (2lb) baby red-skinned potatoes in half widthways. Place in a large bowl with 2 tbsp olive oil, 25g (¾oz) sachet medium peri peri seasoning and 3 crushed cloves garlic, then season; mix well to coat. Taking care, place potatoes in the air fryer basket; at 200°C/400°F, cook for 20 minutes, turning halfway through cooking time, until golden and tender. Drizzle with peri peri sauce for extra heat, if you like.

prep + cook time 30 minutes **serves** 6

FETTA, DILL & BACON POTATOES

Preheat a 7-litre air fryer to 200°C/400°F for 3 minutes. Cut 1kg (2lb) baby red-skinned potatoes into quarters. Place in a large bowl with 2 tbsp olive oil, then season; mix well to coat. Taking care, place potatoes in the air fryer basket; at 200°C/400°F, cook for 20 minutes, turning halfway through cooking time, until golden and tender. Add 150g (4½oz) chopped rindless middle-cut bacon rashers to the air fryer basket for the last 7 minutes of cooking time. Meanwhile, combine 30g (1oz) crumbled fetta, 1 tbsp chopped dill, 2 tbsp whole-egg mayonnaise and ¼ cup sour cream in a large bowl; add potatoes and toss to coat. Top with the crispy bacon and extra dill sprigs.

ASIAN-STYLE WHOLE SNAPPERS

2 x 600g (1¼lb) whole snappers, cleaned
5cm (2in) piece ginger, peeled, julienned
2 cloves garlic, sliced thinly
1 stalk lemongrass, chopped coarsely
1 lime, sliced thinly
2 tbsp kecap manis (sweet soy sauce)
2 tbsp sweet chilli sauce
2 tbsp lime juice
1 tbsp fish sauce
1 tbsp sesame oil
olive oil cooking spray
3 green onions (scallions), sliced thinly
½ cup coriander (cilantro) sprigs
100g (3oz) snow peas, sliced thinly, blanched (see tip)
to serve: lime cheeks

1 Rinse fish under cold running water; pat dry with paper towel. Place each fish on a large piece of greased foil. Using a sharp knife, cut three shallow slits on each side of the fish.

2 Divide three-quarters of the ginger, the garlic, lemongrass and lime slices between the cavities of the fish. Combine kecap manis, sweet chilli sauce, lime juice, fish sauce and sesame oil in a jug. Pour half the sauce mixture over the fish; reserve remaining sauce mixture for serving. Fold foil over fish to seal and form parcels.

3 Preheat a 7-litre air fryer to 200°C/400°F for 3 minutes.

4 Taking care, place the fish parcels, side by side, in the air fryer basket; at 200°C/400°F, cook for 10 minutes.

5 Unwrap foil to expose the top side of the fish; spray with oil. Reset the temperature to 180°C/350°F; cook for a further 10 minutes until fish is cooked through.

6 Meanwhile, combine the green onion, coriander, snow peas and remaining ginger in a bowl.

7 Transfer fish to a large platter, drizzle with remaining sauce mixture and top with green onion mixture. Serve with lime cheeks.

match it Sesame & Chilli-baked Broccolini with Mushrooms, page 160.

prep + cook time 45 minutes
serves 4

TIP To blanch snow peas, place in a heatproof bowl, cover with boiling water and stir until bright green. Drain immediately, then cool under cold running water.

EGGPLANT PARMIGIANA 'MEATBALL' SUBS

1 medium eggplant (400g), peeled,
    cut into 4cm (1½in) pieces
olive oil cooking spray
400g (12½oz) can chickpeas (garbanzo
    beans), drained, rinsed
1 small red onion (100g), chopped finely
2 cloves garlic, crushed
1 tbsp finely chopped rosemary leaves
1¾ cups (140g) finely grated parmesan
1½ cups (150g) packaged breadcrumbs
6 long soft bread rolls (300g)
1 cup (260g) tomato pasta sauce,
    heated
40g (1½oz) baby rocket (arugula) leaves
2 tsp balsamic vinegar

1 Preheat a 5.3-litre air fryer to 200°C/400°F for 3 minutes. Line an oven tray with baking paper.

2 Taking care, place eggplant in the air fryer basket and spray with oil; at 200°C/400°F, cook for 15 minutes until golden and tender.

3 Transfer eggplant to a food processor with chickpeas, onion, garlic, rosemary and 1 cup (80g) of the parmesan; process until combined. Season. Add 1 cup (100g) of the breadcrumbs; pulse until combined. Roll level tablespoons of eggplant mixture into 24 balls, then coat in remaining breadcrumbs; spray generously with oil.

4 Place eggplant balls in the basket; at 200°C/400°F, cook for 20 minutes, turning halfway through cooking time, or until golden and heated through.

5 Split rolls lengthways along the top without cutting all the way through; spread sides with pasta sauce. Fill each roll with four eggplant 'meatballs'. Place rolls in the basket; at 200°C/400°F, cook for 5 minutes.

6 Meanwhile, combine rocket and vinegar in a small bowl.

7 To serve, top 'meatball' subs with remaining parmesan and the rocket salad.

prep + cook time 1 hour
serves 6

LEMON & HERB
PORK
SCHNITZELS

½ cup (75g) plain (all-purpose) flour
2 eggs
⅓ cup (80ml) milk
2 cloves garlic, crushed
2 cups (150g) fresh breadcrumbs
⅓ cup (25g) finely grated parmesan
¼ cup chopped chives
1 tbsp finely chopped lemon thyme
2 tsp finely grated lemon rind
500g (1lb) thin pork leg steaks
olive oil cooking spray
to serve: extra lemon thyme, sea salt
   flakes, aïoli, chips and lemon wedges

1 Place flour in a shallow bowl. Lightly beat eggs, milk and garlic in a second shallow bowl. Combine breadcrumbs, parmesan, chives, thyme and lemon rind in a third shallow bowl. Dust pork in flour, shaking off excess, dip in egg mixture, then coat in breadcrumb mixture. Place schnitzels on a plate. Refrigerate for 30 minutes.
2 Preheat a 7-litre air fryer to 180°C/350°F for 3 minutes.

3 Spray schnitzels generously on both sides with oil. Taking care, place half the schnitzels in the air fryer basket; at 180°C/350°F, cook for 10 minutes, turning halfway through cooking time, until golden and cooked through. Transfer to a plate; cover loosely with foil to keep warm. Repeat cooking with remaining schnitzels.
4 Sprinkle schnitzels with extra thyme and salt flakes. Serve with aïoli, chips and lemon wedges.

prep + cook time 40 minutes (+ refrigeration)
serves 4

MATCH IT Kale, Pear, Smoked Cheddar & Almond Salad, page 132.

RIDICULOUSLY GOOD RIBS

2kg (4lb) American-style pork ribs
olive oil cooking spray
1 cup (280g) barbecue sauce
400g (12½oz) packaged coleslaw mix
1 medium green apple (150g),
    sliced thinly
½ cup (125ml) coleslaw dressing

MARINADE
⅓ cup (80ml) apple cider vinegar
2 tbsp worcestershire sauce
2 tbsp honey
2 cloves garlic, crushed
1 tbsp extra virgin olive oil

DRY SPICE MIXTURE
1 tbsp smoked paprika
¼ tsp chilli powder
1 tsp chilli flakes
1½ tsp onion powder
1½ tsp garlic powder
2 tbsp brown sugar

1 Using a small, sharp knife, remove the layer of membrane from the back of the ribs (or ask the butcher to do this for you). Place ribs in a large saucepan; cover well with water. Bring to the boil over medium heat. Reduce heat to a simmer; cook for 45 minutes or until ribs are almost tender.

2 Meanwhile, combine marinade ingredients in a large bowl and dry spice mixture ingredients in a small bowl. Drain ribs; add to marinade and turn to coat. Remove from marinade and sprinkle with dry spice mixture. Using your hands, rub spices all over ribs; spray with oil.

3 Preheat a 5.3-litre air fryer to 180°C/350°F for 3 minutes.

4 Taking care, arrange ribs in the air fryer basket, standing them up and leaning them against the side of the basket and one another.

Reset the temperature to 160°C/325°F; cook for 20 minutes.

5 Brush ribs with three-quarters of the barbecue sauce; at 160°C/325°F, cook for 10 minutes until tender and glazed.

6 Meanwhile, combine coleslaw mix, apple and dressing in a medium bowl.

7 Cut ribs into serving-sized pieces and brush with remaining barbecue sauce. Serve with coleslaw.

prep it You can prepare the ribs to the end of step 2 a day ahead; refrigerate until required. As the ribs will be chilled, you may need to add an extra 5 minutes to the cooking time.

prep + cook time 1½ hours
serves 4

CORN &
SWEET POTATO
HASH
BROWNS
WITH SAUSAGES

750g (1½lb) chopped orange
    sweet potato
cooking oil spray
2 trimmed corn cobs (500g)
2 green onions (scallions),
    chopped finely
4 breakfast sausages (500g)
½ cup (90g) rice flour
2 eggs
1¾ cups (135g) shredded coconut
to serve: baby spinach leaves
    and tomato chutney

1 Place sweet potato in the basket of a 5.3-litre air fryer and spray with oil; at 180°C/350°F, cook for 20 minutes, turning halfway through cooking time.
2 Taking care, add corn to the basket; at 180°C/350°F, cook for 5 minutes.
3 Transfer sweet potato to a bowl and mash. Cut kernels from corn cob. Add kernels to mash with green onion, then season; mix well.
4 Place sausages in the basket; at 180°C/350°F, cook for 15 minutes until browned and cooked through.
5 Meanwhile, shape heaped ⅓ cups of sweet potato mixture into patties; place on a tray lined with baking paper. Place rice flour in a bowl. Lightly beat eggs in a shallow bowl. Place shredded coconut in a third bowl.

Dust patties in flour, shaking off excess, dip in egg, then coat in coconut. Return to lined tray. Freeze for 10 minutes to set coating. (If not cooking immediately, refrigerate.)
6 Transfer sausages to a plate; cover to keep warm. Spray patties with oil on both sides and place in the basket. Reset the temperature to 160°C/325°F; cook for 10 minutes, turning halfway through cooking time, or until golden brown.
7 Serve sausages with hash browns, baby spinach leaves and tomato chutney.

prep + cook time 1¼ hours (+ refrigeration)
serves 4

TIP To ensure this recipe is gluten free, buy gluten-free sausages and tomato chutney.

TIPS Unfrenched lamb cutlets retain the meat and fat at the bone end of the cutlet. Cooking time may vary depending on the thickness of the lamb cutlets. Cut any thick green beans in half lengthways so they cook in the same time.

LAMB
CUTLETS
WITH MUSTARD
RUB & MINT SAUCE

½ cup (125ml) white wine vinegar
½ cup (110g) caster (superfine) sugar
1 bunch mint, chopped finely
2 tbsp extra virgin olive oil
1 tbsp dijon mustard
1 tbsp wholegrain mustard
1 tbsp maple syrup
1 tbsp finely chopped rosemary
1 tsp cracked black pepper
12 unfrenched lamb cutlets (900g)
   (see tips)
300g (9½oz) green beans, trimmed
   (see tips)

1 To make mint sauce, place vinegar, sugar and ¼ cup (60ml) water in a small saucepan; cook, stirring, over low heat until sugar dissolves. Cool slightly. Stir in mint.

2 Preheat a 7-litre air fryer to 200°C/400°F for 3 minutes.

3 Combine oil, mustards, maple syrup, rosemary and pepper in a large bowl; add lamb and toss to coat.

4 Taking care, place lamb in the air fryer basket; at 200°C/400°F, cook for 6 minutes, without turning, until medium or cooked to your liking (see tips). Transfer to a plate; cover with foil and rest for 2 minutes.

5 Meanwhile, boil, steam or microwave beans until just tender; drain.

6 Serve lamb with mint sauce and green beans.

match it Mustard & Mint Potatoes, page 195.

prep + cook time 25 minutes
serves 4

ROAST BEEF
DINNER
WITH GRAVY

1.5kg (3lb) piece beef scotch fillet
1 tbsp extra virgin olive oil
400g (12½oz) small pickling onions,
  unpeeled, halved
2 tbsp wholegrain mustard
1kg (2lb) butternut pumpkin,
  unpeeled, cut into wedges
1 tbsp thyme leaves
to serve: gravy

1 Preheat a 5.3-litre air fryer to 180°C/350°F for 5 minutes.
2 Tie beef at 2cm (¾in) intervals with kitchen string to form a compact shape; brush with 2 teaspoons of the oil and season.
3 Taking care, place beef and onions in the air fryer basket; at 180°C/350°F, cook for 45 minutes, turning halfway through cooking time, for medium or until cooked to your liking (see Air Fryer Cooking Times for Beef).
4 Transfer beef to a tray and brush with mustard. Cover loosely with foil and rest for 20 minutes. Transfer onions to a plate; cover to keep warm.
5 Meanwhile, brush pumpkin with remaining oil; scatter with thyme and season well. Place pumpkin in the basket; at 180°C/350°F, cook for 20 minutes until tender.
6 Serve sliced beef with onions, pumpkin and gravy.

air fryer cooking times for beef

Per 500g (1lb), cook at 180°C/350°F for:
rare 15–20 minutes
medium 20–25 minutes
well done 25–30 minutes

testing meat

Insert a meat thermometer into the thickest part of the beef. The internal temperature should reach:

rare 55–60°C/130–140°F
medium–rare 60–65°C/140–150°F
medium 65–70°C/150–160°F
medium–well done 70–75°C/160–170°F
well done 75°C/170°F

prep + cook time 1¼ hours
serves 6

SWAP IT Try herbed cream cheese, soft goat's cheese or cheddar instead of fetta.

BACON &
HERBED FETTA
SCRAMBLED
EGGS

30g (1oz) butter, softened
4 eggs
¼ cup (60ml) pouring cream or milk
4 rashers bacon (140g)
4 slices wholegrain bread (180g)
2 small tomatoes (180g), halved
100g (3oz) persian fetta, crumbled
2 tsp thyme leaves

1 Preheat a 5.3-litre air fryer to 180°C/350°F for 3 minutes. Grease a 2-cup (500ml) heatproof dish or bowl generously with the butter.
2 Crack eggs into dish, add cream and season; beat with a fork to combine.
3 Taking care, place dish in the air fryer basket. Place bacon flat and bread beside it, propping it up against the dish, if necessary. Add the tomatoes wherever they will fit; at 180°C/350°F, cook for 10 minutes.

4 Stir eggs with a rubber spatula; cook for a further 3 minutes until egg is almost set, bread is toasted and bacon is crisp. If necessary, cook for longer.
5 To serve, divide toast, bacon and tomato between plates. Spoon scrambled eggs over toast; top with fetta and thyme. Season to taste.

prep + cook time 20 minutes
serves 2

CHEESY BACON PULL-APART

prep + cook time 30 minutes (+ standing)
serves 8

Divide 1 quantity Basic Dough (see recipe opposite) into eight equal portions; roll each portion into a ball. Arrange dough balls, 2cm (¾in) apart, in a greased 23cm (9¼in) round cake pan; cover with plastic wrap. Stand in a warm place for 20 minutes or until doubled in size. Preheat a 7-litre air fryer to 200°C/400°F for 5 minutes. Taking care, place pan in the air fryer basket. Reset the temperature to 170°C/340°F; cook for 15 minutes. Brush bread with 25g (¾oz) melted butter, then sprinkle with ¾ cup grated cheddar and 4 finely chopped rashers shortcut bacon; cook for 8 minutes until bread is golden and cooked through.

TOMATO PESTO FOCACCIA

prep + cook time 40 minutes (+ standing) **serves** 6

Preheat a 7-litre air fryer to 200°C/400°F for 5 minutes. Roll 1 quantity Basic Dough (see recipe opposite) into a 23cm (9¼in) round; place on a large piece of baking paper. Using fingertips, press dimples all over the dough. Trim baking paper so it is 2cm (¾in) larger all around than the dough base. Taking care, use the paper as an aid to lower the focaccia into the air fryer basket. Reset the temperature to 170°C/340°F; cook for 15 minutes. Combine 1 tbsp olive oil and 2 tbsp sun-dried tomato pesto in a small bowl. Spread pesto mixture over focaccia, then sprinkle with 2 cloves sliced garlic and 1 tsp sea salt flakes; cook for 7 minutes until focaccia is golden and cooked through. Top with basil leaves to serve.

GARLIC & PARMESAN TWIST

prep + cook time 40 minutes (+ standing) **serves** 6

Combine 1 tbsp olive oil, 25g (¾oz) melted butter, 3 cloves crushed garlic and 2 tbsp finely chopped chives. Divide 1 quantity Basic Dough (see recipe opposite) into three portions; roll each portion into a 30cm (12in) rope shape. Place ropes, side by side, on a 25cm (10in) square piece of baking paper; pinch at one end to join. Brush with three-quarters of the butter mixture, then sprinkle with 2 tbsp finely grated parmesan. Plait ropes loosely, then pinch end tightly to join; cover with a clean tea towel. Stand in a warm place for 20 minutes or until doubled in size. Preheat a 7-litre air fryer to 200°C/400°F for 5 minutes. Taking care, use the paper as an aid to lower the dough plait diagonally into the air fryer basket. Brush with half the remaining butter mixture. Reset the temperature to 170°C/340°F; cook for 18 minutes. Brush with remaining butter mixture, then sprinkle with 2 tbsp finely grated parmesan; cook for 5 minutes until bread is golden and cooked through.

BREAD

MIXED SEED BUNS

prep + cook time 30 minutes (+ standing) **serves** 8

Combine ¼ cup pepita and sunflower seed mix, 2 tbsp pine nuts, 1 tbsp linseeds and 1 tbsp sesame seeds. Knead half the seed mixture into 1 quantity Basic Dough (see recipe opposite). Divide dough into eight portions; roll each portion into a ball. Place on a tray lined with baking paper; cover with a clean tea towel. Stand in a warm place for 20 minutes or until doubled in size. Preheat a 7-litre air fryer to 200°C/400°F for 5 minutes. Taking care, line the air fryer basket with baking paper. Place the dough balls, 2cm (¾in) apart, in the basket. Cut three shallow slits on the top of each dough ball. Lightly brush tops with 1 lightly beaten egg, then sprinkle with remaining seed mixture. Reset the temperature to 170°C/340°F; cook for 15 minutes until buns are golden and cooked through.

BASIC DOUGH

Combine 600g (1¼lb) packet white bread mix and 2 tsp yeast in a large bowl. Add 1⅓ cups (330ml) lukewarm water; mix to form a dough. Knead dough on a lightly floured surface for 10 minutes (or 6 minutes in an electric mixer fitted with a dough hook) or until dough is smooth and elastic. Return dough to cleaned bowl; cover with plastic wrap. Stand in a warm place for 30 minutes or until doubled in size. Using your fist, punch down on dough to remove air. Knead on a lightly floured surface for 2 minutes or until smooth. Continue with one of the recipe variations to the left.

4 WAYS

cheesy bacon pull-apart

tomato pesto focaccia

garlic & parmesan twist

mixed seed buns

JAPANESE SALMON WITH MISO SAUCE

2 tbsp mirin
2 tbsp cooking sake
2 tbsp soy sauce
800g (1½lb) centre-cut piece
    skinless boneless salmon
8 green onions (scallions), trimmed
2 tsp sesame seeds, toasted

MISO SAUCE
2 tbsp white (shiro) miso
2 tbsp rice wine vinegar
1½ tbsp honey
1½ tbsp soy sauce

1 To make yakitori marinade, combine mirin, sake and soy sauce in a small bowl.
2 To make miso sauce, blend ingredients in a small blender until smooth.
3 Preheat a 5.3-litre air fryer to 160°C/325°F for 3 minutes.
4 Cut salmon into 2cm (¾in) pieces; thread onto six metal or bamboo skewers. Brush all over with the marinade.
5 Taking care, line the air fryer basket with baking paper. Place green onions in the basket; at 160°C/325°F, cook for 5 minutes until tender. Transfer to a platter; cover to keep warm.
6 Place half the skewers in the basket; at 160°C/325°F, cook for 5 minutes or until cooked to your liking. Transfer to platter; cover to keep warm. Repeat cooking with remaining skewers.
7 Serve the salmon and green onions drizzled with miso sauce; sprinkle with sesame seeds.

serve it Serve with microwave brown rice and quinoa and lime cheeks.

prep + cook time 35 minutes
makes 6

SWAP IT The yakitori marinade and miso sauce also work well with large prawns (shrimp). If using prawns, cook them for 5 minutes.

HOISIN PORK WITH
PEANUT RICE

⅓ cup (190g) hoisin sauce

⅓ cup (80ml) salt-reduced soy sauce

2 tbsp chinese cooking wine
(shao hsing)

2 tbsp honey

¼ cup (55g) firmly packed brown sugar

4 cloves garlic, crushed

½ tsp five spice powder

4 x 150g (4½oz) pork scotch fillet steaks

450g (14½oz) packet microwave
jasmine rice

½ cup (70g) unsalted roasted peanuts,
chopped coarsely

2 green onions (scallions), sliced thinly

4 baby cucumbers (240g),
sliced thinly lengthways

to serve: extra hoisin sauce

1 Combine hoisin sauce, soy sauce, cooking wine, honey, sugar, garlic and five spice in a large shallow dish; add pork and turn to coat. Cover dish. Refrigerate for at least 2 hours or overnight.

2 Line the bottom of a 7-litre air fryer pan with foil. Preheat air fryer to 180°C/350°F for 3 minutes.

3 Taking care, place pork in the air fryer basket, reserving the marinade; at 180°C/350°F, cook for 15 minutes, turning and basting pork with reserved marinade halfway through cooking time.

4 Reset the temperature to 200°C/400°F; cook pork for a further 5 minutes, basting with reserved marinade, or until charred and cooked through. Transfer to a dish; cover with foil and rest for 5 minutes.

5 Meanwhile, heat rice following packet directions. Transfer to a medium heatproof bowl; stir in peanuts and half the green onion.

6 Slice pork; serve with rice, cucumber and remaining green onion. Drizzle pork with any cooking juices from the bottom of the air fryer pan and extra hoisin sauce.

prep + cook time 35 minutes
(+ refrigeration)
serves 4

APRICOT & PISTACHIO
STUFFED LEG OF LAMB

½ cup (80g) finely chopped
  dried apricots
¼ cup (60ml) orange juice
30g (1oz) butter, chopped
1 medium onion (150g), chopped finely
1 cup (100g) coarse fresh
  sourdough breadcrumbs
¼ cup (30g) pistachios, roasted,
  chopped finely
2 tbsp finely chopped sage
1.2kg (2½lb) easy-carve lamb leg
1 tbsp olive oil
1 bulb garlic, halved
1 cup (250ml) gravy
to serve: roast potatoes (see tip)
  and broccolini

1 Combine the apricots and orange juice in a bowl; set aside for 20 minutes.

2 Meanwhile, melt butter in a medium frying pan over medium heat; add onion and cook, stirring, for 5 minutes or until soft. Stir in breadcrumbs; cook for 1 minute or until breadcrumbs are golden. Remove from heat; stir in pistachios, sage and apricot mixture.

3 Preheat a 7-litre air fryer to 200°C/400°F for 5 minutes.

4 Untie and unroll lamb; place, skin-side down, on a board. Using a sharp knife, cut three 1cm (½in) deep slits along the length of the lamb to open up the flesh. Press pistachio mixture along the centre of the lamb; roll up to enclose filling. Tie lamb at 2.5cm (1in) intervals with kitchen string to secure. Rub all over with oil and season.

5 Taking care, place lamb and garlic in the air fryer basket. Reset the temperature to 170°C/325°F; cook for 25 minutes. Turn lamb over and cover with foil; cook for a further 25 minutes for medium or until cooked to your liking.

6 Transfer lamb and garlic to a dish; cover loosely with foil and rest for 10 minutes.

7 Serve slices of lamb with garlic, warm gravy, roast potatoes and broccolini.

tip To roast potatoes, cook 1kg (2lb) halved kipfler potatoes tossed in olive oil at 200°C/400°F for 20 minutes, turning halfway through cooking time, until golden and tender. Season with sea salt flakes to serve.

prep + cook time 1 hour 15 minutes (+ standing)
serves 6

TIP While traditionally a brekkie, you can also serve this Middle Eastern dish as a light supper.

WHITE BEAN
SHAKSHUKA

2 tbsp finely chopped coriander
(cilantro) stems
2 green onions (scallions),
chopped finely
½ tsp ground cumin
½ tsp smoked paprika
2 tsp extra virgin olive oil
400g (12½oz) jar arrabbiata pasta sauce
400g (12½oz) can cannellini beans,
drained, rinsed
1 chargrilled capsicum (bell pepper)
(60g), sliced
4 eggs, at room temperature
1 medium avocado (250g), diced
to serve: purple salad leaves and
chargrilled split pitta bread

1 Oil a 3-cup (750ml) 20cm (8in) ovenproof dish; ensure the dish will fit into a 5.3-litre air fryer. (You can also use two large ramekins and increase the eggs to four.)
2 Place coriander stems, green onion, spices and oil in the dish, then place in the air fryer basket; at 180°C/350°F, cook for 3 minutes until fragrant.
3 Taking care, add pasta sauce, beans and capsicum to dish; stir until combined. Cover top of dish with foil; at 180°C/350°F, cook for a further 10 minutes until mixture is hot.

4 Make four indents in the bean mixture and break an egg into each, then season; at 180°C/350°F, cook for 8 minutes until eggs are just set or cooked to your liking.
5 Top shakshuka with avocado and salad leaves. Serve with chargrilled pitta bread.

prep + cook time 25 minutes
serves 2

221

CRACKING PORK BELLY & ASIAN SALAD

1kg (2lb) piece boneless pork belly,
    rind scored (see tips)
1 tbsp salt flakes
½ tsp chinese five spice powder
olive oil cooking spray
1 lebanese cucumber (130g),
    sliced thinly lengthways
1 small red onion (100g), sliced thinly
¼ medium wombok (napa cabbage)
    (250g), shredded
1 cup thai basil leaves
1 cup coriander (cilantro) leaves
2 cups (60g) baby spinach
2 long red chillies, seeded, sliced thinly
1 green onion (scallion), sliced thinly
1 lime (65g), cut into wedges

GINGER DRESSING
1 stalk lemongrass, chopped finely
1 tbsp finely grated ginger
1½ tbsp soy sauce
1½ tbsp lime juice
1 tbsp sesame oil
1 tbsp rice wine vinegar
1 tbsp caster (superfine) sugar

1 Preheat a 5.3-litre air fryer to 180°C/350°F for 3 minutes.

2 Pat pork dry with paper towel. Combine half the salt flakes and the five spice; rub into pork rind.

3 Taking care, place pork in the air fryer basket and spray with oil. Reset temperature to 200°C/400°F; cook for 25 minutes until pork skin crackles.

4 Reset the temperature to 160°C/325°F; cook for a further 30 minutes until pork is tender, or an internal temperature of 70–75°C/160–170°F is reached on a meat thermometer. (Cover pork with foil if overbrowning.)

5 Meanwhile, to make ginger dressing, whisk ingredients in a small bowl.

6 Layer cucumber, red onion, wombok, herbs, spinach and chilli on a platter.

7 Thickly slice pork and place on top of salad. Scatter with green onion and sprinkle with remaining salt flakes; drizzle with the dressing. Serve with lime wedges.

tips A Stanley knife is the best tool for scoring the pork rind; alternatively, you can get the butcher to do it for you. As soon as you get home, place the pork on a tray, uncovered, in the fridge for up to 2 days to dry the rind out – this will assist with crackling the rind.

prep + cook time 1¼ hours
serves 4

GREEN CURRY CHICKEN WITH PICKLED RADISH

2 tbsp thai green curry paste
1 tbsp extra virgin olive oil
1 tbsp fish sauce
1 tbsp lime juice
1 tbsp brown sugar
4 chicken thigh cutlets (800g),
    skin on
to serve: microwave coconut rice and
    finely chopped green onion (scallion)

PICKLED RADISH

¼ cup (60ml) rice wine vinegar
1 tsp brown sugar
½ tsp sea salt flakes
6 mixed radishes (220g), trimmed,
    sliced thinly (see tip)

1 To make pickled radish, combine vinegar, sugar and salt flakes in a small bowl; add ¼ cup (60ml) cold water and stir to combine. Add radishes; mix to combine. Set aside until required.
2 Preheat a 7-litre air fryer to 180°C/350°F for 3 minutes.
3 Combine curry paste, oil, fish sauce, lime juice and sugar in a large bowl; add chicken and turn to coat.
4 Taking care, place chicken, skin-side down, in the air fryer basket; at 180°C/350°F, cook for 20 minutes, turning after 8 minutes, or until golden and cooked through. (There will be a little bit of smoke in the initial 5–7 minutes of cooking; however, this will stop with further cooking.)

5 Serve chicken on coconut rice, topped with chopped green onion and drained pickled radish.

tip We used a mixture of red and watermelon radishes for the pickle.

prep + cook time 35 minutes
serves 4

225

CHICKEN
PARMIS

3 chicken breast fillets (600g)
½ cup (75g) plain (all-purpose) flour
2 eggs
1 clove garlic, crushed
1½ cups (110g) panko (japanese)
   breadcrumbs
1 tsp sweet paprika
2 tsp finely grated lemon rind
1 tbsp finely chopped flat-leaf parsley
cooking oil spray
1 cup (280g) tomato pasta sauce
160g (5oz) mozzarella, sliced
¼ cup (20g) finely grated parmesan
to serve: baby rocket (arugula),
   roasted truss tomatoes (see tip)
   and lemon wedges

1 Cut chicken fillets in half horizontally to make six pieces. Place chicken between two sheets of plastic wrap; pound gently with a rolling pin until even in thickness.

2 Place flour in a small bowl and season. Lightly beat eggs, garlic and 1 tablespoon water in a second bowl. Place breadcrumbs, paprika, lemon rind and parsley in a third bowl. Dust chicken in flour, shaking off excess, dip in egg, then coat in breadcrumb mixture. Spray schnitzels generously on both sides with oil.

3 Preheat a 5.3-litre air fryer to 180°C/350°F for 3 minutes.

4 Taking care, place three schnitzels in the air fryer basket; at 180°C/350°F, cook for 12 minutes until golden brown and cooked through. Transfer to a tray; cover to keep warm. Repeat cooking with remaining schnitzels.

5 Return three schnitzels to the basket. Top each with 2 tablespoons pasta sauce; scatter with half the mozzarella and parmesan; at 180°C/350°F, cook for 8 minutes until cheeses are melted and bubbling. Repeat with remaining schnitzels, pasta sauce, mozzarella and parmesan.

6 Serve chicken parmis with rocket, roasted tomatoes and lemon wedges.

prep + cook time 1 hour
makes 6

TIP To roast truss tomatoes, add them to the edge of the basket with the schnitzels in step 5; cook for 6 minutes.

CHEAT'S SAUSAGE CASSOULET

500g (1lb) thick pork sausages
olive oil cooking spray
1 tbsp extra virgin olive oil
1 medium onion (150g), chopped finely
2 bacon rashers (160g), sliced thinly
2 cloves garlic, crushed
1 medium red capsicum (bell pepper)
    (200g), chopped coarsely
1 medium zucchini (120g),
    chopped coarsely
250g (8oz) baby roma tomatoes
½ cup (125ml) dry red wine
1½ cups (390g) tomato pasta sauce
3 sprigs thyme
400g (12½oz) can butter beans,
    drained, rinsed
1½ cups (105g) coarse fresh
    sourdough breadcrumbs
⅓ cup (25g) grated gruyère cheese
⅓ cup chopped flat-leaf parsley
to serve: sea salt flakes

1 Preheat a 7-litre air fryer to 200°C/400°F for 3 minutes.

2 Spray sausages with oil. Taking care, place sausages in the air fryer basket; at 200°C/400°F, cook for 8 minutes, turning halfway through cooking time, or until browned.

3 Meanwhile, heat oil in a large frying pan over medium-high heat; cook onion and bacon, stirring, for 5 minutes or until onion is softened and bacon is crisp. Add garlic, capsicum and zucchini; cook, stirring, for 4 minutes or until vegetables are lightly browned. Add tomatoes and wine; bring to the boil. Add pasta sauce and thyme; return to the boil.

4 Transfer sausages to a board and chop coarsely; add to tomato mixture with butter beans. Transfer mixture to a deep 20cm (8in) round ovenproof dish.

5 Taking care, wipe the air fryer basket clean; place the dish in the basket. Reset the temperature to 180°C/350°F; cook for 8 minutes.

6 Meanwhile, combine breadcrumbs, gruyère and parsley in a bowl.

7 Top cassoulet with breadcrumb mixture, spray with oil, then press crumbs down firmly; at 180°C/350°F, cook for 5 minutes until breadcrumbs are golden.

8 Sprinkle cassoulet with salt flakes to serve.

prep + cook time 40 minutes
serves 4

SOUTHERN FRIED CHICKEN

1.6kg (3¼lb) whole chicken (see tip)
1 cup (250ml) buttermilk
1 egg, beaten lightly
1¼ cups (185g) plain (all-purpose) flour
2 tsp smoked paprika
1 tsp garlic powder
1 tsp onion flakes
1 tsp dried oregano
1 tsp sea salt flakes
1 tsp ground cumin
½ tsp chilli powder
olive oil cooking spray
to serve: extra sea salt flakes,
    mayonnaise and hot sauce

1 Using a sharp knife, cut chicken into eight pieces. Make two deep slits through the thickest part of the meat to the bone in each chicken piece.

2 Combine buttermilk and egg in a large bowl, then season; add chicken and turn to coat. Cover bowl. Refrigerate for 6 hours or overnight.

3 Combine flour, paprika, garlic powder, onion flakes, oregano, salt, cumin and chilli powder in a large bowl; season.

4 Working with one piece of chicken at a time, drain excess buttermilk mixture, then roll in flour mixture to coat. Repeat with remaining chicken and flour mixture; spray generously all over with oil.

5 Preheat a 7-litre air fryer to 200°C/400°F for 3 minutes.

6 Taking care, line the air fryer basket with a silicone mat, if available (see page 11). Place chicken in the basket; at 200°C/400°F, cook for 10 minutes.

7 Turn chicken over. Reset the temperature to 180°C/350°F; cook for 10 minutes or until crisp and cooked through. (The breast pieces may cook a little quicker than the thighs and legs.)

8 Sprinkle chicken with extra salt flakes. Serve with mayonnaise swirled with a little hot sauce.

prep + cook time 40 minutes (+ refrigeration)
serves 4

TIP You could also use 1.6kg (3¼lb) chicken pieces on the bone; you may need to adjust the cooking time depending on the pieces.

AIR
BAKE

The air fryer isn't just about savoury food, it's also brilliant at sweet treats too. Make all your favourite baked recipes, such as cakes, puddings, muffins, brownies, cookies, muesli bars and more.

CHOCOLATE CAKE
WITH FUDGE ICING

125g (4oz) butter, softened
1 tsp vanilla extract
¾ cup (165g) caster (superfine) sugar
2 eggs
1¼ cups (185g) self-raising flour
½ cup (50g) cocoa powder
½ cup (125ml) milk

FUDGE ICING
50g (1¾oz) butter, chopped
⅓ cup (75g) firmly packed brown sugar
1 tbsp milk
1 cup (160g) icing (confectioners') sugar
2 tbsp cocoa powder

1 Preheat a 7-litre air fryer to 160°C/325°F for 5 minutes. Grease a deep 20cm (8in) round cake pan; line base and side with baking paper.
2 Beat butter, vanilla, sugar, eggs, sifted flour and cocoa, and milk in a large bowl with an electric mixer on low speed until combined. Increase speed to medium; beat for 3 minutes or until mixture is smooth and paler in colour. Spoon mixture into cake pan. Cover pan with a piece of greased foil.
3 Taking care, place cake pan in the air fryer basket; at 160°C/325°F, cook for 1 hour until a skewer inserted into the centre comes out clean. Remove from the basket. Leave cake in pan for 10 minutes before turning, top-side up, onto a wire rack to cool.

4 Meanwhile, to make fudge icing, stir butter, brown sugar and milk in a small saucepan over low heat until sugar dissolves. Remove from heat. Sift icing sugar and cocoa into a small bowl; gradually whisk in hot butter mixture until smooth. Cover bowl. Refrigerate for 40 minutes or until icing thickens.
5 Beat icing with a wooden spoon until spreadable. Spread top of cooled cake with fudge icing.

prep + cook time 1¼ hours (+ refrigeration)
serves 12

TIP Make sure you are wearing a long-sleeved top while piping the churros mixture into the hot air fryer basket, as this will protect you from touching the hot sides.

CHURROS
WITH CHOCOLATE
SAUCE

60g (2oz) butter
pinch sea salt flakes
½ cup (125ml) cold water
⅓ cup (75g) caster (superfine) sugar
½ cup (75g) plain (all-purpose) flour
2 eggs, beaten lightly
olive oil cooking spray
1 tsp ground cinnamon
125g (4oz) dark (semi-sweet)
    chocolate, chopped
½ cup (125ml) thickened (heavy) cream

1 Bring butter, salt, the cold water and 1 tablespoon of the sugar to the boil in a medium saucepan. Add sifted flour; beat with a wooden spoon over high heat until mixture comes away from the base and side of the pan to form a smooth ball. Transfer to a small bowl; beat in egg, in two batches, with a wooden spoon until mixture becomes glossy. Spoon into a piping bag fitted with a 2cm (¾in) fluted tube.

2 Preheat a 7-litre air fryer to 180°C/350°F for 3 minutes.

3 Spray the air fryer basket with oil. Taking care, pipe four 10cm (4in) lengths of batter, 5cm (2in) apart, into the basket (see tip); at 180°C/350°F, cook for 12 minutes until golden and crisp. Repeat cooking with remaining batter to make a total of 8 churros.

4 Meanwhile, to make cinnamon sugar, combine cinnamon and remaining sugar in a shallow bowl. Immediately place hot churros in cinnamon sugar and toss to coat.

5 To make chocolate sauce, place chocolate and cream in a small saucepan over low-medium heat; stir until smooth and combined.

6 Serve churros with warm chocolate sauce.

prep + cook time 45 minutes
makes 8

LEMON CURD SCONES

2⅓ cups (375g) self-raising flour
⅓ tsp baking powder
pinch fine salt
2 tbsp raw sugar
300ml buttermilk
¼ cup (80g) lemon curd
olive oil cooking spray
to serve: jam and whipped cream

1 Sift flour, baking powder, salt and sugar into a large bowl. Make a well in the centre; pour in combined buttermilk and lemon curd. Using a flat-bladed knife, gently stir until dough just comes together.
2 Turn dough out onto a lightly floured work surface. Using your hands, knead briefly. Pat out until dough is 3cm (1¼in) thick.
3 Using a floured cutter, cut 5.5cm (2¼in) rounds from dough. Press scraps of dough together until 3cm (1¼in) thick. Repeat cutting to get a total of 9 scones. Brush top of scones with any buttermilk left in the carton or 1 tablespoon of milk.
4 Preheat a 7-litre air fryer to 180°C/350°F for 3 minutes.
5 Spray the air fryer basket with oil. Taking care, place scones, side by side, in the basket. Reset the temperature to 160°C/325°F; cook for 17 minutes.
6 Serve warm scones with jam and cream.

prep + cook time 35 minutes
makes 9

SERVE IT You can also serve
the scones with lemon curd and
whipped cream, if you like.

CARROT
CAKE

3 eggs
1⅓ cups (295g) firmly packed
 brown sugar
1 cup (250ml) extra virgin olive oil
3 cups (720g) coarsely grated carrot
1 cup (120g) coarsely chopped walnuts
2½ cups (375g) self-raising flour
½ tsp bicarbonate of soda (baking soda)
2 tsp mixed spice
250g (8oz) cream cheese, softened
¾ cup (240g) lemon curd
to serve: zested lemon rind (see tip)

1 Preheat a 5.3-litre air fryer to 160°C/325°F for 5 minutes. Grease a deep 20cm (8in) round springform cake pan; line base and side with baking paper. Ensure the pan will fit into the air fryer.

2 Beat eggs, sugar and oil in a bowl with an electric mixer until thick and creamy. Stir in carrot and walnuts, then sifted dry ingredients. Spoon mixture into cake pan; cover with foil.

3 Taking care, place cake pan in the air fryer basket; at 160°C/325°F, cook for 1¼ hours until a skewer inserted into the centre comes out clean. Remove from the basket. Leave cake in pan for 10 minutes before turning, top-side up, onto a wire rack to cool.

4 Meanwhile, beat cream cheese in a small bowl with an electric mixer until softened. Add ½ cup (160g) lemon curd; beat until just combined.

5 Spread top of cake with lemon curd cream cheese; dollop with remaining lemon curd and scatter with zested lemon rind.

tip Use a zesting tool to create thin strips of rind; if you don't have one, peel large pieces of rind, avoiding the pith, then cut into thin strips.

prep + cook time 1½ hours (+ cooling)
serves 12

APPLE & STRAWBERRY CRUMBLE

250g (8oz) strawberries

3 large red apples (600g)

1 tsp vanilla bean paste

2 tbsp orange juice

2 tbsp maple syrup

⅓ cup (25g) flaked natural almonds, roasted

to serve: icing (confectioners') sugar and vanilla ice-cream

SPICED CRUMBLE TOPPING

1 cup (120g) almond meal

¾ cup (65g) rolled oats

3 tsp ground ginger

1 tsp mixed spice

2 tbsp maple syrup

75g (2½oz) cold butter, chopped finely

1 To make spiced crumble topping, place ingredients in a medium bowl. Using fingertips, rub mixture together until it forms small clumps.

2 Halve strawberries. Peel, core and coarsely chop apples. Combine apple, strawberries, vanilla, orange juice and maple syrup in a large bowl.

3 Preheat a 5.3-litre air fryer to 180°C/350°F for 3 minutes.

4 Grease four 10cm (4in) ovenproof dishes; ensure the dishes will fit into the air fryer. Divide fruit mixture among dishes (fruit will reduce down during cooking).

5 Taking care, place dishes in the air fryer basket; at 180°C/350°F, cook for 10 minutes until fruit is almost tender.

6 Top fruit with crumble topping. Cover dishes with foil; at 180°C/350°F, cook for 10–15 minutes until crumble is golden and fruit is bubbling.

7 Top crumbles with flaked almonds and dust with icing sugar. Serve with ice-cream.

prep + cook time 35 minutes
serves 4

KEEP IT Uncooked spiced crumble topping can be frozen for up to 3 months. Use frozen and bake for 20 minutes.

PEANUT BUTTER
BROWNIES

125g (4oz) butter, chopped
200g (6½oz) dark chocolate
   (45% cocoa), chopped
½ cup (110g) caster (superfine) sugar
½ cup (160g) caramel Top 'n' Fill
¼ cup (70g) crunchy peanut butter
2 eggs, beaten lightly
1 cup (150g) plain (all-purpose) flour
¼ cup (35g) self-raising flour
1 tbsp cocoa powder

1 Stir butter and chocolate in a medium saucepan over low heat until just smooth. Remove from heat; stir in sugar. Cool for 10 minutes.

2 Preheat a 7-litre air fryer to 160°C/325°F for 5 minutes. Grease a 20cm (8in) square cake pan; line base and sides with baking paper.

3 Microwave Top 'n' Fill for 30 seconds or until softened; stir in the peanut butter.

4 Stir egg into chocolate mixture, then sifted flours and cocoa. Spread half the brownie mixture into cake pan; dollop with half the peanut butter mixture.

Gently spread remaining brownie mixture over the top, then dollop with remaining peanut butter mixture. Using a skewer, swirl the peanut butter mixture through the brownie mixture. Cover pan tightly with foil.

5 Taking care, place cake pan in the air fryer basket; at 160°C/325°F, cook for 25 minutes.

6 Remove foil; cook for a further 10 minutes or until brownie is just set on top. Remove from the basket. Leave brownie in pan to cool.

7 Cut brownie into 12 pieces.

prep + cook time 55 minutes
makes 12

CARAMELISED
ONION, DILL
& CARAWAY
SAUSAGE ROLLS

500g (1lb) minced (ground) pork
1 cup (100g) packaged breadcrumbs
1 egg, beaten lightly
2 cloves garlic, crushed
¼ cup finely chopped dill
1 tbsp caraway seeds
½ cup (150g) caramelised onion relish
2 tsp malt vinegar
3 sheets frozen puff pastry, just thawed
2 egg yolks
1 tsp caraway seeds, extra
cooking oil spray
to serve: HP sauce or barbecue sauce

1 Preheat a 5.3-litre air fryer to 180°C/350°F for 3 minutes.

2 Combine pork mince, breadcrumbs, egg, garlic, dill, caraway seeds, relish and vinegar in a large bowl; season well.

3 Cut pastry sheets in half. Spoon or pipe pork mixture in a line through the centre of each pastry piece; roll pastry over to enclose filling. Cut each roll into four pieces; place, seam-side down, on a tray lined with baking paper. Combine egg yolks and 1 teaspoon water in a small bowl. Brush pastry with egg and sprinkle with extra caraway seeds.

4 Spray the air fryer basket with oil. Taking care, place 8 sausage rolls in the basket; at 180°C/350°F, cook for 15 minutes until puffed and cooked through. Transfer to a wire rack. Repeat cooking two more times with the remaining sausage rolls.

5 Serve hot sausage rolls with sauce.

prep it Sausage rolls can be prepared to the end of step 3 a day ahead; refrigerate until ready to bake.

keep it Sausage rolls can be frozen in an airtight container for up to 3 months.

prep + cook time 1 hour
makes 24

SPANAKOPITA
COBB LOAF

18cm (7¼in) round sourdough cob loaf
cooking oil spray
200g (6½oz) frozen spinach, thawed
300g (9½oz) sour cream
½ cup (60g) grated cheddar
40g (1½oz) packet french onion
   soup mix
¼ cup (75g) caramelised onion relish
50g (1½oz) fetta, crumbled
to serve: baby carrots, baby cucumbers,
   cherry tomatoes and witlof

1 Preheat a 5.3-litre air fryer to 160°C/325°F for 3 minutes.

2 Slice the top from the cob loaf, ensuring the base is about 4cm (1½in) high. Neatly cut out the bread centre in one piece, leaving a 5mm (¼in) thick shell. Cut bread centre into eight wedges to make dippers. Spray the inside of the cob shell, the cut-side of the lid and the dippers with oil.

3 Taking care, place the cob shell in the air fryer basket; at 160°C/325°F, cook for 3 minutes until golden and crisp. Transfer to a tray. Repeat cooking two more times with the bread lid and dippers.

4 Meanwhile, squeeze out excess liquid from thawed spinach. Combine spinach, sour cream, cheddar, soup mix, relish and 2 tablespoons water in a medium bowl. Spoon mixture into cob shell; scatter with fetta.

5 Place the cob loaf in the basket; at 160°C/325°F, cook for 10 minutes until filling is heated through.

6 Serve cob loaf with bread dippers, baby carrots, baby cucumbers, cherry tomatoes and witlof for dipping. Tear the bread lid into pieces to make extra dippers.

prep + cook time 30 minutes
serves 8

STRAWBERRY POP TARTS

250g (8oz) strawberries, chopped finely
2 tbsp strawberry jam
1 tbsp cornflour (cornstarch)
4 sheets frozen shortcrust pastry,
   just thawed
1 egg, beaten lightly
½ cup (80g) icing (confectioners') sugar
2 tsp cold water
pink food colouring, to tint
to serve: 100's & 1,000's

1 Combine strawberries, jam and cornflour in a small bowl. Cut each pastry sheet into six 8cm x 10cm (3¼in x 4in) rectangles. Place a level tablespoon of strawberry mixture in the centre of half the pastry rectangles. Brush edges of pastry with a little egg. Cover filling with remaining pastry rectangles; using a fork, press edges together to seal.

2 Preheat a 7-litre air fryer to 180°C/350°F for 3 minutes.

3 Taking care, place half the tarts in the air fryer basket; at 180°C/350°F, cook for 12 minutes, turning after 10 minutes of cooking time, until pastry is golden and cooked. Transfer to a wire rack to cool. Repeat cooking with remaining tarts.

4 Combine icing sugar, the cold water and food colouring in a small bowl. Spoon icing over cooled tarts; sprinkle immediately with 100's & 1,000's. Stand until icing sets.

prep + cook time 35 minutes (+ standing)
makes 12

TIPS You will need 2 large bananas for this recipe. Muffins are best eaten on the day of making.

FREE-FORM BANANA PECAN MUFFINS

1 cup (150g) self-raising flour
½ cup (110g) firmly packed brown sugar
1 egg, beaten lightly
1 tsp vanilla extract
¼ cup (60ml) grapeseed oil
¼ cup (60ml) milk
¾ cup mashed banana (see tips)
27 pecan halves (40g)

1 Triple layer 27 paper muffin cases to make nine thick cases.

2 Combine flour and sugar in a large bowl. Whisk egg, vanilla, oil and milk in a medium bowl; add to dry ingredients, stirring until just combined. Fold banana into mixture until just combined. Divide mixture evenly among muffin cases.

3 Preheat a 7-litre air fryer to 160°C/325°F for 3 minutes.

4 Taking care, place muffin cases in the air fryer basket, then top each with three pecan halves; at 160°C/325°F, cook for 17 minutes until a skewer inserted into the centre of a muffin comes out clean. Transfer to a wire rack to cool.

prep + cook time 35 minutes
makes 9

5-INGREDIENT CELEBRATION CAKE

8 eggs, at room temperature
440g (14oz) Nutella
⅓ cup boiling water
½ cup (75g) self-raising flour
110g (3½oz) Nutella, extra
1½ tbsp boiling water, extra
1 cup (250ml) thickened cream,
    whipped
125g (4oz) raspberries
to serve: cocoa powder (optional)

1 Grease a 19cm (7¾in) round non-stick springform cake pan; line base with baking paper.

2 Beat 4 eggs with an electric mixer on high speed for 10 minutes or until tripled in volume.

3 Place 220g (7oz) Nutella and 2 tablespoons boiling water in a microwave-safe bowl. Microwave on HIGH (100%) for 20 seconds. Whisk until smooth.

4 Preheat a 5.3-litre air fryer to 160°C/325°F for 3 minutes.

5 Whisk a quarter of the beaten egg into the melted Nutella until combined, then fold in ¼ cup (35g) flour. Gently fold in remaining beaten egg in two batches. Pour mixture into cake pan. Cover pan with a piece of greased foil; pierce the foil.

6 Taking care, place cake pan in the air fryer basket; at 160°C/325°F, cook for 30 minutes until a skewer inserted into the centre comes out clean.

Remove from the basket. Remove foil and reserve for the second cake. Leave cake in pan for 15 minutes before turning out onto a wire rack covered with baking paper to cool completely. Peel away the lining paper.

7 Repeat steps 1–6 to make a second cake.

8 Place extra Nutella in a small bowl; stir in extra boiling water to loosen. Spread over top of one of the cooled cakes, then top with the second cake. Spread top of cake with cream and scatter with raspberries; dust with cocoa, if you like.

prep it Undecorated cakes will keep in an airtight container at room temperature for up to 3 days.

prep + cook time 1½ hours (+ cooling)
serves 12

TIP Allow turnovers to cool slightly before eating so you don't scorch your mouth.

NUTELLA
TURNOVERS

2 sheets frozen puff pastry, just thawed
½ cup (165g) Nutella
½ cup (60g) finely chopped
   roasted hazelnuts
1 egg, beaten lightly

1 Preheat a 7-litre air fryer to 200°C/400°F for 3 minutes.

2 Cut each pastry sheet into nine 8cm (3¼in) squares. Spoon 1½ teaspoons Nutella and 1 teaspoon hazelnuts onto the centre of each square. Brush edges of pastry with a little egg. Fold pastry over to enclose filling and form a triangle. Using a fork, press edges together to seal.

3 Taking care, place half the turnovers in the air fryer basket; at 200°C/400°F, cook for 8 minutes until pastry is golden and cooked. Transfer to a wire rack. Repeat cooking with remaining turnovers.

4 Serve turnovers warm.

prep + cook time 30 minutes
makes 18

BERRY FRANGIPANE GALETTE

---

1 cup (150g) plain (all-purpose) flour
2 tbsp caster (superfine) sugar
60g (2oz) chilled butter, chopped
1 egg yolk
2 tbsp almond meal
150g (4½oz) frozen mixed berries
2 tsp cornflour (cornstarch)
to serve: icing (confectioners') sugar
    and ice-cream

FRANGIPANE FILLING
60g (2oz) butter, softened
¼ cup (55g) caster (superfine) sugar
1 tsp vanilla extract
1 egg yolk
⅔ cup (80g) almond meal
1½ tbsp plain (all-purpose) flour

1 To make pastry, process flour, sugar and butter in a food processor until mixture resembles fine breadcrumbs. Add egg yolk; process until dough just comes together. Turn out onto a work surface and shape into a disc; wrap in plastic wrap. Refrigerate for 30 minutes.

2 Meanwhile, to make frangipane filling, beat butter, sugar and vanilla in a small bowl with an electric mixer until pale and creamy. Beat in egg yolk until combined. Stir in almond meal and flour until combined.

3 Preheat a 7-litre air fryer to 180°C/350°F for 5 minutes.

4 Roll pastry between two sheets of baking paper until 3mm (⅛in) thick. Using a plate or cake pan, cut out a 25cm (10in) round from pastry; discard offcuts. Sprinkle almond meal over pastry round, then evenly spread with frangipane, leaving a 3cm (1in) border. Toss berries in cornflour to coat, shaking off excess; scatter over frangipane. Fold pastry border up and over filling.

5 Taking care, using the paper as an aid, lower the galette into the air fryer basket, then cover basket tightly with foil; at 180°C/350°F, cook for 30 minutes.

6 Remove foil. Reset the temperature to 160°C/325°F; cook for a further 15–18 minutes or until pastry is golden and frangipane is cooked through. Taking care, using the paper as an aid, lift the galette from the basket.

7 Dust the galette with icing sugar and serve with ice-cream.

prep + cook time 1 hour 10 minutes (+ refrigeration)
serves 6

KEEP IT Muesli bars
will keep in an airtight
container for up to 2 weeks.

MUESLI BARS

2 cups (180g) rolled oats
⅓ cup (50g) sunflower seeds
¼ cup (50g) pepitas (pumpkin
    seed kernels)
125g (4oz) dried apricots
2 tbsp white chia seeds
2 tbsp boiling water
⅓ cup (25g) desiccated coconut
100g (3oz) butter, chopped
⅓ cup (75g) firmly packed brown sugar
2 tbsp honey
½ tsp ground cinnamon

1 Process 1 cup (90g) oats until the consistency of desiccated coconut. Add sunflower seeds and pepitas; pulse briefly until a few are coarsely chopped. Transfer mixture to a large bowl. Process apricots, chia seeds and the boiling water until finely chopped; add to the bowl with coconut.

2 Stir butter, sugar, honey and cinnamon in a medium saucepan over low heat until sugar dissolves and mixture is smooth; stir into oat mixture until combined, then stir in remaining oats.

3 Remove the basket from the pan of a 5.3-litre air fryer and place on a sheet of baking paper; trace around the base. Cut out shape 2cm (¾in) larger than the marked tracing. Grease basket and line with the paper cut-out.

4 Press oat mixture very firmly over the paper; use the base of a glass or an offset spatula to compact the mixture. Insert the basket back into the air fryer pan; at 140°C/285°F, cook for 40 minutes.

5 Remove the basket from the air fryer pan and place on a wire rack to cool completely. Using the paper as an aid, lift the slice from the basket and transfer to a board; cut into 12 bars.

prep + cook time 1 hour
makes 12

APPLEY PIE ROLLS

400g (12½oz) can pie fruit apple slices, chopped
¼ cup (40g) sultanas
1½ tbsp caster (superfine) sugar
½ tsp ground cinnamon
1½ tbsp almond meal
8 x 21.5cm (8¾in) frozen spring roll wrappers, thawed (see tip)
olive oil cooking spray
to serve: icing (confectioners') sugar and vanilla ice-cream

1 Combine apple, sultanas, sugar, cinnamon and almond meal in a medium bowl.
2 Place a spring roll wrapper on a clean work surface. Place 2 level tablespoons of filling in a line a third up from the bottom edge, leaving a 4cm (1½in) border on each side. Fold bottom of wrapper over filling once, fold in the sides, then roll up to enclose filling; brush the join with a little water to seal. Repeat with remaining spring roll wrappers and filling.
3 Preheat a 7-litre air fryer to 200°C/400°F for 3 minutes.
4 Spray rolls generously all over with oil. Taking care, place rolls in the air fryer basket; at 200°C/400°F, cook for 15 minutes until golden brown.
5 Dust rolls with icing sugar and serve with ice-cream.

prep + cook time 35 minutes
makes 8

TIP You can find spring roll wrappers in the freezer section of the supermarket.

KEEP IT Cookies will keep in an airtight container for up to 2 weeks.

BASIC VANILLA BUTTER COOKIES

125g (4oz) butter, softened
½ cup (110g) caster (superfine) sugar
1 tsp vanilla extract
1 egg yolk
1¼ cups (185g) plain (all-purpose) flour
2 tbsp caster (superfine) sugar, extra
to serve: icing (confectioners') sugar

1 Beat butter, sugar and vanilla in a small bowl with an electric mixer until light and fluffy. Beat in egg yolk until combined. Sift flour, in two batches, into butter mixture; mix well.
2 Knead dough on a lightly floured surface until smooth. Using your hands, shape dough into a 25cm (10in) long log. Place extra caster sugar on a plate; roll log in the sugar. Wrap log in baking paper. Freeze for 1 hour or until firm.
3 Remove log from the freezer. Stand for 10 minutes. Slice into 15 x 1.5cm (¾in) thick rounds.
4 Preheat a 7-litre air fryer to 160°C/325°F for 5 minutes.

5 Taking care, line the air fryer basket with baking paper. Place half the cookies, 2cm (¾in) apart, in the basket (place remaining cookies in the fridge until needed); at 160°C/350°F, cook for 12 minutes until golden. Remove the basket from the air fryer pan. Leave cookies in the basket for 10 minutes before transferring to a wire rack to cool completely. Repeat cooking with remaining cookies.
6 Dust cookies with icing sugar.

prep + cook time 40 minutes (+ freezing, standing & cooling)
makes 15

TRIPLE-CHOC

Add ⅓ cup (80g) each milk, dark and white chocolate chips into 1 quantity Basic Vanilla Butter Cookies recipe (page 265) just before adding the flour in step 1. Roll level tablespoons of mixture into balls. Flatten balls until 1cm (½in) thick. Freeze for 20 minutes. Bake as recipe directs in steps 4 and 5.

tip You could also use 180g (5½oz) hand-chopped chocolate of a single type, if preferred.

COOKIES

SPICED MAPLE

Add 1 tsp ground mixed spice into 1 quantity Basic Vanilla Butter Cookies recipe (page 265) when adding the flour in step 1. Continue with the recipe from step 2. To make maple icing, combine ¾ cup sifted icing (confectioners') sugar, 1½ tbsp maple syrup and 3 tsp water; beat with a wooden spoon until icing is smooth and a pouring consistency. Drizzle icing on top of cooled cookies.

4 WAYS

ORANGE & PECAN

Add 1 tsp finely grated orange rind and ½ cup chopped toasted pecans into 1 quantity Basic Vanilla Butter Cookies recipe (page 265) just before adding the flour in step 1. Continue with the recipe from step 2.

LEMON & CRANBERRY

Add 1 tsp finely grated lemon rind and ½ cup (65g) dried cranberries into 1 quantity Basic Vanilla Butter Cookies recipe (page 265) just before adding the flour in step 1. Continue with the recipe from step 2.

orange & pecan
cookies

triple-choc
cookies

lemon & cranberry
cookies

spiced maple
cookies

CHOCOLATE LAVA CAKES

25g (¾oz) butter, softened
2 tbsp cocoa powder
155g (5oz) dark (semi-sweet)
  chocolate, chopped coarsely
125g (4oz) butter, extra, chopped
2 eggs
2 egg yolks
⅓ cup (75g) caster (superfine) sugar
¼ cup (35g) plain (all-purpose) flour
to serve: extra cocoa powder
  and coffee ice-cream

1 Grease six ¾-cup (180ml) ovenproof dishes (ramekins or metal dariole moulds) with softened butter; dust with cocoa, shaking off excess.
2 Stir chocolate and extra butter in a small saucepan over low heat until smooth. Cool for 10 minutes. Transfer mixture to a large bowl.
3 Beat eggs, egg yolks and sugar in a small bowl with an electric mixer until thick and creamy. Fold egg mixture and sifted flour into barely warm chocolate mixture. Spoon mixture into dishes.
4 Preheat a 7-litre air fryer to 180°C/350°F for 3 minutes.

5 Taking care, place dishes in the air fryer basket; at 180°C/350°F, cook for 10–12 minutes. Remove from the basket. Leave cakes in the dishes for 1 minute before gently inverting onto serving plates.
6 Dust cakes with extra cocoa and serve immediately with ice-cream.

tips These cakes should be served shortly after they come out of the air fryer. If they are allowed to sit for longer than 1 minute, the gooey centre will firm up and the chocolate won't ooze out when they're cut. Warning: the melted chocolate centre will be hot, so take care when biting into the cake.

prep + cook time 30 minutes (+ cooling)
serves 6

CHOCOLATE CANNOLI WITH HAZELNUT CREAM

1 cup (150g) plain (all-purpose) flour
1 tbsp cocoa powder
1 tbsp caster (superfine) sugar
1 egg
1 egg yolk
1 tbsp marsala
2 tsp olive oil
2 tsp cold water
1 egg white, beaten lightly
olive oil cooking spray
to serve: icing (confectioners') sugar
    and fresh raspberries

HAZELNUT CREAM
1 cup (250ml) thickened (heavy) cream
2 tbsp icing (confectioners') sugar
125g (4oz) mascarpone
¼ cup (85g) Nutella

1 Process flour, cocoa and sugar until just combined. Add egg, egg yolk, marsala, oil and the cold water; process until dough starts to come together. Turn out onto a lightly floured surface; knead until smooth. Divide dough in half and shape into two discs; wrap in plastic wrap. Refrigerate for 1 hour.
2 Roll one dough disc on a lightly floured surface until 2mm thick (alternatively, roll dough through a pasta machine). Using a 10cm (4in) round cutter, cut out six rounds, re-rolling the scraps if necessary. Wrap each round around an ungreased metal cannoli mould (see tip), overlapping ends slightly. Brush ends with a little egg white to secure (ensure you don't get egg white on the moulds, as otherwise the dough will stick to them once cooked). Repeat with remaining dough disc to make 12 cannoli shells in total.
3 Preheat a 7-litre air fryer to 200°C/400°F for 3 minutes.
4 Spray cannoli all over with oil. Taking care, line the air fryer basket with baking paper. Place cannoli in the basket; at 200°C/400°F, cook for 7 minutes, turning halfway through cooking time, or until golden. Using tongs, transfer to a plate to cool slightly. Carefully remove moulds from warm cannoli. Cool.
5 Meanwhile, to make hazelnut cream, beat cream and icing sugar in a small bowl with an electric mixer until soft peaks form. Add mascarpone and Nutella; beat for 20 seconds or until just combined. Spoon cream mixture into a piping bag fitted with a 1cm (½in) plain nozzle. Pipe hazelnut cream into cooled cannoli shells.
6 Dust cannoli with icing sugar. Serve with raspberries.

tip Cannelloni pasta shells can be used instead of metal cannoli moulds; however, you will need to grease them first. Ensure you wrap dough rounds loosely around the pasta shells to make removing them easier.

prep + cook time 45 minutes (+ refrigeration)
makes 12

KEEP IT Tart will keep in an airtight container in the fridge for up to 3 days.

TANGY LEMON TART

125g (4oz) butter, chopped coarsely
¼ cup (40g) icing (confectioners') sugar
1¼ cups (185g) plain (all-purpose) flour
3 eggs
1 cup (220g) caster (superfine) sugar
2 tsp finely grated lemon rind
½ cup (125ml) lemon juice
cooking oil spray
1 medium lemon (140g), sliced thinly
2 tbsp caster (superfine) sugar, extra
to serve: extra icing (confectioners')
   sugar, to dust

1 Preheat a 5.3-litre air fryer to 180°C/350°F for 3 minutes. Grease a 20cm (8in) loose-based tart pan.

2 Beat butter and icing sugar in a small bowl with an electric mixer until smooth. Stir in 1 cup (150g) of the flour until a dough forms. Press mixture evenly over base and up the side of the tart pan. Fold a length of foil into a long strip; place under tart pan to act as a sling.

3 Taking care, lower tart pan, on the sling, into the air fryer basket; at 180°C/350°F, cook for 10 minutes.

4 Using the back of a spoon, press crust back down over the base and up the side of the tart pan; cook for a further 8 minutes until tart base is dry and lightly golden.

5 Meanwhile, to make filling, place eggs, caster sugar, remaining flour, the lemon rind and juice in a medium saucepan; whisk continuously over medium heat until mixture boils and thickens.

6 Pour hot filling mixture into a jug, then pour over the hot tart base in the basket. Reset the temperature to 160°C/325°F; cook for 3–5 minutes until filling is set. Using the foil sling as an aid, lift from the basket and place on a wire rack. Leave tart in pan to cool.

7 Meanwhile, spray the basket with oil. Sprinkle lemon slices with extra caster sugar and place in the basket; at 160°C/325°F, cook for 6 minutes until caramelised.

8 To serve, top tart with caramelised lemon slices and dust with extra icing sugar.

prep + cook time 45 minutes
serves 8

MEGA CARROT CAKE MUFFINS

2 cups (240g) almond meal
2 tbsp chia seeds
1 tsp gluten-free baking powder
½ tsp bicarbonate of soda (baking soda)
1 tsp ground cinnamon
1 tbsp ground ginger
3 eggs
¼ cup (60ml) extra virgin olive oil
¾ cup (110g) coconut sugar
2 tsp vanilla extract
1 large zucchini (150g)
1 large carrot (180g)
1 large apple (200g)
½ cup (120g) smooth ricotta
¼ cup (40g) natural almonds, chopped

1 Preheat a 5.3-litre air fryer to 160°C/325°F for 3 minutes. Triple layer 18 muffin wraps to make six thick wraps.

2 Combine almond meal, chia seeds, baking powder, bicarb and spices in a large bowl. Whisk eggs, oil, coconut sugar and vanilla in a medium bowl; add to dry ingredients, stirring until just combined.

3 Coarsely grate zucchini, carrot and apple into a medium bowl. Using your hands, pick up handfuls of the zucchini mixture and squeeze very firmly to remove excess liquid. Fold zucchini mixture into almond mixture until just combined. Divide muffin mixture evenly among muffin wraps.

4 Taking care, place muffin wraps in the air fryer basket; at 160°C/325°F, cook for 5 minutes.

5 Cover top of muffins with a piece of foil; cook for a further 25 minutes.

6 Top each muffin with a spoonful of ricotta and scatter with chopped almonds; at 160°C/325°F, cook for 5 minutes until ricotta is browned and a skewer inserted into the centre of a muffin comes out clean. Transfer to a wire rack to cool.

keep it Muffins will keep in an airtight container in the fridge for up to 1 week, or they can be frozen for up to 2 months.

prep + cook time 45 minutes
makes 6

SPICED DOUGHNUT BITES

250g (8oz) packet doughnut bites mix
2 tbsp vegetable oil
1 egg
¼ cup (60ml) milk
2 tsp finely grated orange rind
½ tsp ground nutmeg
40g (1½oz) butter, melted

1 Preheat a 7-litre air fryer to 180°C/350°F for 3 minutes. Grease two 12-hole (1 tablespoon/20ml) mini muffin pans.

2 Place doughnut mix in a medium bowl. Whisk oil, egg and milk in a jug until combined. Gently stir milk mixture into doughnut mix until just combined (do not over-mix). Divide doughnut mixture among pan holes.

3 Taking care, lower one muffin pan into the air fryer basket; at 180°C/350°F, cook for 8 minutes until doughnuts are golden and a skewer inserted into the centre of one comes out clean. Remove from the air fryer. Leave doughnuts in pan for 5 minutes before turning out onto a wire rack to cool slightly. Repeat cooking with remaining muffin pan.

4 Meanwhile, place cinnamon sugar mix from the packet of doughnut bites mix in a medium bowl. Add orange rind and nutmeg; mix well.

5 Lightly brush warm doughnut bites with melted butter, then toss in the cinnamon sugar mixture.

6 Serve doughnut bites warm.

variation For spiced Nutella doughnut bites, spoon half the doughnut mixture into pan holes, top each with ½ teaspoon Nutella, then spoon the remaining doughnut mixture over Nutella. Continue with recipe from step 3.

prep + cook time 35 minutes
makes 24

LEMON CURD & RASPBERRY BREAD & BUTTER PUDDING

250g (8oz) crusty sourdough bread,
  sliced thickly
½ cup (160g) lemon curd
1 cup (250ml) thickened (heavy) cream
¾ cup (180ml) milk
3 eggs
¼ cup (55g) caster (superfine) sugar
1 tsp vanilla extract
125g (4oz) frozen raspberries
to serve: extra lemon curd

1 Grease a 1.5-litre (6-cup), 20cm (8in) round baking dish; ensure the dish will fit into a 7-litre air fryer.
2 Spread bread slices thickly with lemon curd. Arrange bread, curd-side up, in dish.
3 To make custard, combine cream and milk in a microwave-safe jug; heat in microwave on HIGH (100%) for 2 minutes or until warm. Whisk eggs, sugar and vanilla in a bowl until combined; gradually whisk in warm cream mixture until combined.
4 Pour custard over bread slices in dish; scatter with raspberries. Using a spatula, press bread down gently to submerge in the custard. Stand for 5 minutes. Cover dish tightly with foil.

5 Preheat air fryer to 150°C/300°F for 5 minutes.
6 Taking care, place dish in the air fryer basket; at 150°C/300°F, cook for 30 minutes.
7 Remove foil. Reset the temperature to 160°C/325°F; cook for a further 12 minutes until golden and just set. Remove from the basket. Leave pudding for 5 minutes to cool slightly.
8 Serve pudding dolloped with extra lemon curd.

prep + cook time 1 hour
serves 12

TIP Homemade pesto
can be replaced with
¼ cup (65g) bottled basil
or sun-dried tomato pesto.

CHEESY PESTO SCROLLS

1 cup firmly packed basil leaves

1 clove garlic, chopped

2 tbsp pine nuts, toasted

2 tbsp finely grated parmesan

¼ cup (60ml) extra virgin olive oil

1 tbsp lemon juice

2 cups (300g) self-raising flour

1 tsp fine salt

1 tbsp caster (superfine) sugar

50g (1½oz) cold butter, chopped coarsely

¾ cup (180ml) milk, approximately

1 cup (120g) grated pizza cheese

1 To make pesto, process basil, garlic, pine nuts and parmesan in a food processor until chopped finely. With motor operating, gradually add combined oil and lemon juice until pesto is almost smooth; season.

2 Sift flour and salt into a medium bowl; stir in sugar. Using your fingers, rub in butter. Add enough milk to form a soft, sticky dough. Turn out onto a lightly floured sheet of baking paper; knead lightly until smooth. Sprinkle paper with more flour, if necessary. Roll dough out into a 30cm x 40cm (12in x 16in) rectangle.

3 Spread dough evenly with the pesto; scatter over pizza cheese. Roll dough up tightly from a long side to form a log; place log in the freezer for 10 minutes to firm slightly.

4 Preheat a 7-litre air fryer to 160°C/325°F for 5 minutes.

5 Using a serrated knife, trim ends off the log; cut into 12 slices.

6 Taking care, line the air fryer basket with baking paper. Place scrolls, cut-side up, in the basket, then cover basket tightly with foil; at 160°C/325°F, cook for 10 minutes.

7 Remove foil; cook for a further 10 minutes until scrolls are golden and cooked through.

8 Serve scrolls warm or cold.

prep + cook time 50 minutes (+ freezing)

makes 12

PASSIONFRUIT BUTTERMILK CAKE

125g (4oz) butter
1 cup (220g) caster (superfine) sugar
2 tsp vanilla extract
2 eggs
2 cups (300g) self-raising flour
⅔ cup (160ml) buttermilk
¾ cup (180ml) passionfruit pulp
  (see tip)
1½ cups (240g) icing
  (confectioners') sugar

1 Preheat a 7-litre air fryer to 160°C/325°F for 5 minutes. Grease a deep 20cm (8in) round springform cake pan; line base and side with baking paper. Ensure the pan will fit into the air fryer.

2 Beat butter, caster sugar and vanilla in a bowl with an electric mixer until thick and creamy. Beat in eggs, one at a time, until combined. Fold in flour, buttermilk and ¼ cup of the passionfruit pulp. Spoon mixture into cake pan; cover with foil.

3 Taking care, place cake pan in the air fryer basket; at 160°C/325°F, cook for 30 minutes.

4 Remove foil; cook for a further 30 minutes or until a skewer inserted into the centre comes out clean. Remove from the basket. Leave cake in pan for 10 minutes before turning out onto a wire rack to cool.

5 To make passionfruit icing, combine icing sugar and remaining passionfruit pulp in a small bowl. Spread top of cooled cake with icing.

tip You will need about 9 passionfruit for this recipe.

prep + cook time 1¼ hours (+ cooling)
serves 12

BANANA FRITTERS WITH SALTED CARAMEL SAUCE

15g (½oz) butter, chopped
1½ cups (110g) panko (japanese) breadcrumbs
½ cup (40g) desiccated coconut
½ cup (75g) plain (all-purpose) flour
2 eggs
¼ cup (60ml) milk
4 ripe bananas, halved lengthways
to serve: vanilla ice-cream

SALTED CARAMEL SAUCE
½ cup (125ml) thickened (heavy) cream
½ cup (110g) firmly packed brown sugar
30g (1oz) butter, chopped
1 tsp sea salt flakes

1 Melt butter in a medium frying pan over medium-high heat. Add breadcrumbs and coconut; cook, stirring, for 2 minutes or until breadcrumbs are browned lightly. Transfer to a plate to cool.

2 Place flour on a plate. Whisk eggs and milk together in a medium shallow bowl. Dust bananas in flour, shaking off excess, dip in egg mixture, then coat in breadcrumb mixture. Refrigerate for 15 minutes.

3 Preheat a 7-litre air fryer to 180°C/350°F for 3 minutes.

4 Taking care, place fritters in the air fryer basket; at 180°C/350°F, cook for 8 minutes, turning halfway through cooking time, or until golden.

5 Meanwhile, to make salted caramel sauce, stir ingredients, except salt, in a small saucepan over low heat, without boiling, until sugar dissolves. Bring to the boil, then reduce heat; simmer for 3 minutes or until thickened slightly. Remove from heat and stir in salt.

6 Serve fritters with ice-cream, drizzled with salted caramel sauce.

prep + cook time 25 minutes (+ refrigeration)
serves 4

285

BANANA BREAD

125g (4oz) butter, softened
1 cup (220g) firmly packed brown sugar
1 tsp vanilla extract
2 eggs
1½ cups (350g) mashed ripe banana
   (see tip)
¼ cup (60ml) maple syrup
1⅔ cups (250g) plain (all-purpose) flour
1 tsp baking powder
1 tsp bicarbonate of soda (baking soda)
1½ tsp ground cinnamon
¼ tsp salt flakes
½ cup (25g) coarsely chopped
   roasted walnuts
2 small bananas (130g each),
   halved lengthways
2 tbsp demerara sugar
to serve: ricotta and honey

1 Grease a 10.5cm x 20cm (4in x 8in) loaf pan; line base and sides with baking paper, ensuring paper sits flush with the rim.

2 Beat butter, brown sugar and vanilla in a medium bowl with an electric mixer until pale and fluffy. Beat in eggs, one at a time, until just combined, then mashed banana and maple syrup. Sift over flour, baking powder, bicarb, cinnamon and salt. Add walnuts; stir with a large spoon until combined. Spoon mixture into loaf pan; smooth surface.

3 Preheat a 5.3-litre air fryer to 160°C/325°F for 3 minutes.

4 Taking care, place loaf pan in the air fryer basket; at 160°C/325°F, cook for 10 minutes.

5 Place banana halves, cut-side up, on top of bread. Cover loaf pan with foil and pierce the foil; at 160°C/325°F, cook for 40 minutes.

6 Remove foil; cook for another 5 minutes until a skewer inserted into the centre comes out clean. Remove from the basket. Leave bread in pan for 10 minutes before turning, top-side up, onto a wire rack to cool. Sprinkle top with demerara sugar while hot.

7 Serve slices of banana bread topped with ricotta and drizzled with honey.

tip You will need 3 large bananas to make 1½ cups mashed banana.

prep + cook time 1¼ hours
serves 8

BERRY BAKED PANCAKE

olive oil cooking spray
1 cup (150g) plain (all-purpose) flour
¼ cup (55g) caster (superfine) sugar
¼ tsp bicarbonate of soda (baking soda)
⅔ cup (160ml) buttermilk
1 egg, beaten lightly
2 tsp vanilla extract
30g (1oz) butter, melted
50g (1½oz) blueberries
50g (1½oz) raspberries
to serve: icing (confectioners') sugar
    and maple syrup

1 Preheat a 7-litre air fryer to 180°C/350°F for 3 minutes. Spray a non-stick 18cm (7¼in) round, 2.5cm (1in) deep pizza pan (see tip) with oil.

2 Place flour, sugar and bicarb in a large bowl; stir to combine. Whisk buttermilk, egg, vanilla and butter in a medium jug. Add buttermilk mixture to flour mixture, stirring until just combined. Spread mixture into pizza pan and smooth top; scatter with berries, pressing them in gently.

3 Taking care, place pizza pan in the air fryer basket; at 180°C/350°F, cook for 15 minutes until a skewer inserted into the centre comes out clean.

4 Dust warm pancake with icing sugar and serve with maple syrup.

tip Many air fryers come with an accessory pack that includes a pizza pan.

prep + cook time 30 minutes
serves 4

COOKIE PIE

220g (7oz) frozen shortcrust
    pastry case
75g (2½oz) butter, softened
⅔ cup (150g) firmly packed brown sugar
1 egg
1 tsp vanilla extract
1 cup (150g) self-raising flour
pinch salt
¼ cup (45g) dark (semi-sweet)
    chocolate chips
¾ cup (110g) assorted chocolates
    (see tip)
to serve: icing (confectioners') sugar

1 Preheat a 5.3-litre air fryer to 170°C/340°F for 3 minutes.
2 Cover frozen pastry case with foil, then weigh foil down with two metal spoons. Taking care, place pastry case in the air fryer basket; at 170°C/340°F, cook for 10 minutes until pastry is lightly golden and dry. Transfer to a board to cool.
3 Meanwhile, to make chocolate chip cookie filling, beat butter, sugar, egg and vanilla in a small bowl with an electric mixer for 6 minutes or until light and creamy. Stir in sifted flour and salt, then chocolate chips.
4 Fill pastry case with the filling; smooth surface. Press assorted chocolates into top of pie. Place pie in the basket; cover with foil.
5 Reset the temperature to 160°C/325°F; cook for 30 minutes until a skewer inserted into the centre of the pie comes out with a few crumbs attached and top is browned and puffed.
6 Serve pie warm or cool, dusted with icing sugar.

tip For pie one (top left) we used Smarties, Rolos (caramel-filled chocolate rolls) and freckles. For pie two (top right) we used sliced Liquorice Allsorts, Rolos, unicorn confetti and strawberry Pocky sticks. For pie three (bottom) we used Smarties, Rolos, chocolate-coated pretzels, cake decorations and mini milk arrowroot letters (biscuits).

serve it Serve with scoops of vanilla ice-cream.

prep + cook time 1 hour
makes 1 pie (serves 6)

GLOSSARY

baking powder a raising agent consisting mainly of two parts cream of tartar to one part bicarbonate of soda.

bicarbonate of soda a raising agent.

breadcrumbs

fresh bread, usually white, processed into crumbs.

packaged fine-textured, crunchy purchased white breadcrumbs.

panko also known as japanese breadcrumbs. Available in larger pieces and fine crumbs; both have a lighter crunchier texture than Western-style breadcrumbs, with a delicate, pale golden colour.

brioche French in origin; a rich, yeast-leavened, cake-like bread made with butter and eggs.

broccolini a cross between broccoli and chinese kale; long asparagus-like stems with a long loose floret, both edible. Resembles broccoli in looks but is milder and sweeter in taste.

buk choy also known as bok choy, pak choy, chinese white cabbage or chinese chard; has a fresh, mild mustard taste. Use both stems and leaves. Baby buk choy is smaller and more tender than buk choy.

buttermilk originally the term given to the slightly sour liquid left after butter was churned from cream, today it is made from no-fat or low-fat milk to which specific bacterial cultures have been added during the manufacturing process.

capers grey-green buds of a warm climate shrub (usually Mediterranean); sold either dried and salted or pickled in a vinegar brine. Baby capers are very small and have a fuller flavour. Rinse well before using.

cheese

cheddar the most common cow's milk 'tasty' cheese; should be aged, hard and have a pronounced bite.

fetta Greek in origin; a crumbly goat's or sheep's milk cheese with a sharp, salty taste. Ripened and stored in salted whey.

gruyère a Swiss cheese with small holes and a nutty, slightly salty flavour.

mascarpone a cultured cream product made in much the same way as yoghurt. Whitish to creamy yellow in colour with a soft, creamy texture and a rich, sweet, slightly acidic taste.

mozzarella soft, spun-curd cheese that originated in southern Italy where it was traditionally made from water-buffalo milk. Now, generally made from cow's milk, it is the most popular pizza cheese.

parmesan also called parmigiano; a hard, grainy cow's milk cheese. The curd is salted in brine for a month then aged for up to 2 years.

pizza a blend of grated mozzarella, cheddar and parmesan cheeses.

ricotta a soft, sweet, moist, white cow's milk cheese, low in fat and slightly grainy in texture. It roughly translates as 'cooked again' and refers to its manufacture from a whey that is itself a by-product of other cheese-making.

chia seeds contain protein and all the essential amino acids, as well as being fibre rich and containing a wealth of vitamins, minerals and antioxidants.

chilli

cayenne pepper a long, thin-fleshed, extremely hot red chilli, usually sold dried and ground.

flakes also sold as crushed chilli; dehydrated, deep-red, extremely fine slices and whole seeds.

green any unripened chilli; also some particular varieties that are ripe when green, such as jalapeño, habanero, poblano or serrano.

long red available both fresh and dried; a generic term used for any moderately hot, long (6–8cm), thin chilli.

powder the Asian variety is the hottest, made from dried ground thai chillies; can be used instead of fresh in the proportion of ½ teaspoon chilli powder to 1 medium chopped fresh red chilli.

chinese cooking wine also known as shao hsing or chinese rice wine; made from fermented rice, wheat, sugar and salt with a 13.5 per cent alcohol content. Inexpensive and found in Asian food shops. If you can't find it, replace with mirin or sherry.

GLOSSARY

coconut

cream obtained commercially from the first pressing of the coconut flesh alone, without the addition of water; the second pressing (less rich) is sold as coconut milk. Available in cans and cartons at supermarkets.

desiccated concentrated, dried, unsweetened and finely shredded coconut flesh.

shredded unsweetened thin strips of dried coconut flesh.

coriander also called cilantro or chinese parsley; a bright-green leafy herb with a pungent aroma and taste. Both stems and roots are used: wash well before chopping. Coriander seeds are dried and sold whole or ground; neither tastes remotely like the fresh leaf.

cornflour (cornstarch) available made from corn or wheat (wheaten cornflour gives a lighter texture in cakes); used as a thickening agent in cooking.

couscous a fine grain-like cereal product made from semolina.

cream

pouring also known as pure cream.

thickened (heavy) a whipping cream containing thickener; has a minimum fat content of 35 per cent.

cumin the dried seed of a plant related to the parsley family. Has a spicy, almost curry-like flavour. Available as seeds or ground.

curry pastes

thai green paste the hottest of the traditional Thai pastes; contains chilli, garlic, onion, salt, lemongrass, spices and galangal.

thai red paste a base for many Thai dishes; usually consists of red chilli, garlic, sea salt, lemongrass, turmeric and shrimp paste.

tikka paste a medium-mild paste of chilli, coriander, cumin, lentil flour, garlic, ginger, turmeric, fennel, cloves, cinnamon and cardamom.

dukkah an Egyptian spice blend made with roasted nuts and aromatic spices.

fennel seeds dried seeds with a licorice flavour.

five spice powder a ground spice blend usually consisting of cloves, cinnamon, star anise, sichuan pepper and fennel seeds.

harissa a North African paste made from dried red chillies, garlic, olive oil and caraway seeds; can be used as a rub for meat, an ingredient in sauces and dressings, or eaten as a condiment.

lemongrass a tall, clumping, lemon-smelling and -tasting, sharp-edged grass; the white part of the stem is used, finely chopped, in cooking.

lentils (red, brown, yellow) dried pulses often identified by and named after their colour; also known as dhal.

mushrooms

button small, cultivated white mushrooms with a mild flavour. When a recipe in this book calls for an unspecified type of mushroom, use button.

oyster also known as abalone; grey-white mushrooms shaped like a fan with a smooth texture and subtle oyster-like flavour.

portobello large, fully grown cremini or baby bella mushrooms with a brown or beige cap that averages about 15cm (6in) in diameter, with distinctive dark brown or black gills and a woody stem under the cap; have an earthy flavour and meaty texture.

swiss brown also known as cremini or roman mushrooms; light brown mushrooms with a full-bodied flavour.

mustard

dijon also called french. Pale brown, creamy, distinctively flavoured, fairly mild French mustard.

wholegrain also known as seeded mustard. A French-style coarse-grain mustard made from crushed mustard seeds and Dijon-style french mustard. Works well with cold meats and sausages.

nutmeg a strong and pungent spice ground from the dried nut of an evergreen tree native to Indonesia. Usually found ground but the flavour is more intense from a whole nut, so it's best to grate your own.

GLOSSARY

oil

coconut extracted from the coconut flesh. The best quality is virgin coconut oil, which is the oil pressed from the dried coconut flesh and doesn't include the use of solvents or other refining processes.

cooking spray we use an olive oil cooking spray in this book, unless otherwise indicated.

olive made from ripened olives. Extra virgin and virgin are the first and second press, respectively, and are considered the best; reference to 'extra light' or 'light' is to taste not fat levels.

sesame made from roasted, crushed, white sesame seeds; a flavouring rather than a cooking medium.

vegetable oils sourced from plant rather than animal fats.

onions

green also known as scallion or, incorrectly, shallot; an immature onion picked before the bulb has formed. Have a long, bright-green edible stalk.

red also known as spanish, red spanish or bermuda onion; a sweet-flavoured, large, purple-red onion.

shallots also called french shallots, golden shallots or eschalots; small, brown-skinned, elongated members of the onion family. Grow in tight clusters like garlic.

pak choy similar to baby buk choy, except the stem is a very pale green rather than white and the top is less leafy.

paprika ground, dried, sweet red capsicum (bell pepper); there are many types available, including sweet, hot, mild and smoked.

pepitas the pale green kernels of dried pumpkin seeds; can be bought plain or salted.

pine nuts also called pignoli; not a nut but the small, cream-coloured kernel from pine cones.

polenta also known as cornmeal; a flour-like cereal made of ground corn (maize). Also the name of the dish made from it.

sauces

fish called nuoc naam (Vietnamese) or naam pla (Thai); the two are almost identical. Made from pulverised salted fermented fish; has a pungent smell and strong taste. Use to your taste.

hoisin a thick, sweet and spicy Chinese paste made from salted fermented soy beans, onions and garlic.

kecap manis (ketjap manis); a thick soy sauce with added sugar and spices. The sweetness is derived from the addition of molasses or palm sugar.

oyster Asian in origin, this rich, brown sauce is made from oysters and their brine, cooked with salt and soy sauce and thickened with starches.

soy made from fermented soy beans. Several variations are available in most supermarkets and Asian food stores. We use Japanese soy sauce unless otherwise indicated.

sweet chilli a mild sauce made from red chillies, sugar, garlic and vinegar.

worcestershire thin, dark-brown spicy sauce developed by the British when in India; used as a seasoning for meat, gravies and cocktails, and as a condiment.

sesame seeds black and white are the most common of this small oval seed; however, there are also red and brown varieties.

spring roll wrappers also known as egg roll wrappers; they come in various sizes and can be purchased fresh or frozen. Made from a delicate wheat-based pastry, they can be used for making gow gee and samosas as well as spring rolls.

sumac a purple-red, astringent spice ground from berries growing on shrubs flourishing wild around the Mediterranean; adds a tart, lemony flavour to food. Available from spice shops and major supermarkets.

taco seasoning mix a packaged seasoning meant to duplicate the Mexican sauce made from oregano, cumin, chillies and other spices.

tahini a rich sesame seed paste used in most Middle Eastern cuisines.

turmeric related to ginger; adds a golden-yellow colour to food.

CONVERSION CHART

MEASURES

One Australian metric measuring cup holds approximately 250ml; one Australian metric tablespoon holds 20ml; one Australian metric teaspoon holds 5ml. North America, New Zealand and the United Kingdom use a 15ml tablespoon.

The difference between one country's measuring cups and another's is within a two- or three-teaspoon variance and will not affect your cooking results. All cup and spoon measurements are level.

The most accurate way of measuring dry ingredients is to weigh them.

When measuring liquids, use a clear glass or plastic jug with metric markings.

We use extra-large eggs with an average weight of 60g each.

DRY MEASURES

metric	imperial
15g	½oz
30g	1oz
60g	2oz
90g	3oz
125g	4oz (¼lb)
155g	5oz
185g	6oz
220g	7oz
250g	8oz (½lb)
280g	9oz
315g	10oz
345g	11oz
375g	12oz (¾lb)
410g	13oz
440g	14oz
470g	15oz
500g	16oz (1lb)
750g	24oz (1½lb)
1kg	32oz (2lb)

LIQUID MEASURES

metric	imperial
30ml	1 fluid oz
60ml	2 fluid oz
100ml	3 fluid oz
125ml	4 fluid oz
150ml	5 fluid oz
190ml	6 fluid oz
250ml	8 fluid oz
300ml	10 fluid oz
500ml	16 fluid oz
600ml	20 fluid oz
1000ml (1 litre)	1¾ pints

LENGTH MEASURES

metric	imperial
3mm	⅛in
6mm	¼in
1cm	½in
2cm	¾in
2.5cm	1in
5cm	2in
6cm	2½in
8cm	3in
10cm	4in
13cm	5in
15cm	6in
18cm	7in
20cm	8in
22cm	9in
25cm	10in
28cm	11in
30cm	12in (1ft)

OVEN TEMPERATURES

The oven temperatures below are for conventional ovens; if you are using a fan-forced oven, reduce the temperature by 20 degrees.

	°C (Celsius)	°F (Fahrenheit)
Very slow	120	250
Slow	150	300
Moderately slow	160	325
Moderate	180	350
Moderately hot	200	400
Hot	220	425
Very hot	240	475

Measurements for cake pans are approximate only. Using same-shaped cake pans of a similar size should not affect the outcome of your baking. We measure the inside top of the cake pan to determine size.

INDEX

INDEX

FIRST PUBLISHED IN 2022 BY ARE MEDIA BOOKS, AUSTRALIA. REPRINTED IN 2022, 2023 (TWICE).

Are Media

Chief Executive Officer
Jane Huxley

Are Media Books

Group Publisher
Nicole Byers

Editorial & Food Director
Sophia Young

Books Director
David Scotto

Creative Director
Hannah Blackmore

Managing Editor
Stephanie Kistner

Senior Designer
Kelsie Walker

Food Editor
Sophia Young

Senior Editor
Chantal Gibbs

Photographers
James Moffatt, Nic Gossage, Craig Wall

Stylists
Olivia Blackmore, Kate Brown

Photochefs
Rebecca Lyall, Clare Maguire,
Sophia Young, Jun Chen

Printed in China by
C&C Offset Printing

A catalogue record for this
book is available from the
National Library of Australia.
ISBN 978-1-92586-689-6 (paperback)

© Are Media Pty Limited 2022
ABN 18 053 273 546

Published by Are Media Books,
a division of Are Media Pty Limited,
54 Park St, Sydney; GPO Box 4088,
Sydney, NSW 2001, Australia
Ph +61 2 9282 8000
www.awwcookbooks.com.au

International rights enquiries
internationalrights@aremedia.com.au

Order Books
Phone 1300 322 007 (within Australia)

Or order online at
www.awwcookbooks.com.au

Send recipe enquiries to
recipeenquiries@aremedia.com.au

 womensweeklyfood   @womensweeklyfood

TRUSTED BRANDS USED IN OUR TEST KITCHEN